Deep and Safety Stops including Ascent Speed and Gradient Factors

Description

A study into the current knowledge, tests and practices of "Deep Stops" and Gradient Factors, including current decompression profile practices. To stop or not to stop, and how deep.

By Anton Swanepoel

Deep and Safety Stops, including Ascent Speed and Gradient Factors

I think we took this deep stop thing a bit too far.

By Anton Swanepoel

Rita and Tino de Rijk, Grand Cayman

Introduction

To stop or not, that remains an unanswered question, a question that came from the 1800s with even Paul Bert wondering about it.

The first question one should ask before one can argue about deep stops, is what are deep stops actually? Then one has to ask, how are these stops calculated?

There are probably as many ways to calculate and execute "Deep Stops" as there are ways to calculate decompression.

This book looks at the research done and current understandings of deep stops, both for and against deep stops. The book's aim is not to advocate or discredit the use of deep stops, but rather to be neutral and provide the reader with the most up to date knowledge, research and methods used by various groups, from military to recreational diving. The reader is shown the risks of both incorporating deep stops or not into their dive profile and it is up to the reader to decide if using deep stops is of any benefit in addition to how the user will calculate and execute those stops.

This book also looks at safety stops, ascent speed, descent speed and Gradient Factors and how they affect your decompression schedule.

Welcome to open mind diving.

About the Author

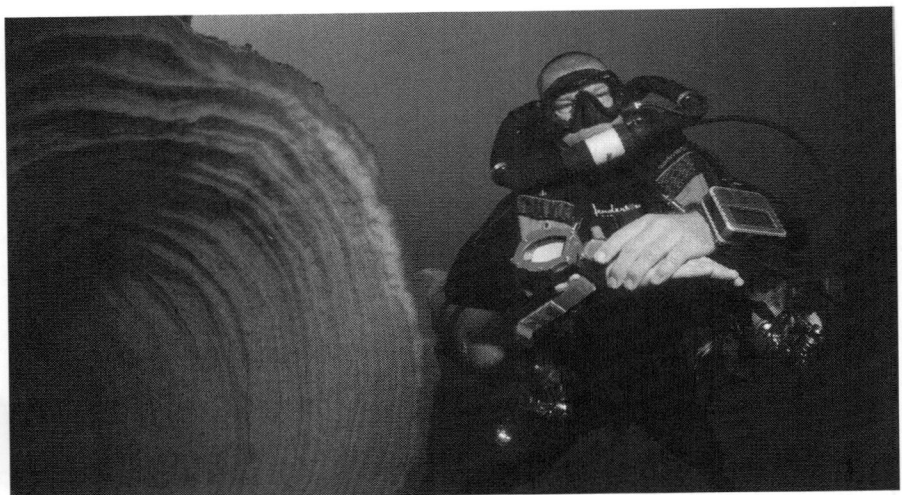

Author at 200 ft, Cayman Islands, Grand Cayman.
Photo taken by Robert Hew

Anton Swanepoel is a diving instructor for IANTD, TDI, NAUI and PADI. He is an OC Tri-Mix instructor and a Tri-Mix gas blender instructor. He has a passion for wreck, cave and deep diving.

Although he dives both CCR and OC, his passion is in OC. Working as a technical instructor in a busy dive centre in the Caribbean, he gets to live his passion. He has dove OC in excess of 400 ft and loves to share his passion with all.

The thoughts expressed in this book are those of the author alone and not of any agency he is an instructor for. Although the author teaches and dives tri-mix and decompression, he is not a research scientist, the material in this book was sourced from various research papers, books, internet articles, e-mail and talks with doctors, research scientists and decompression specialists. The author's hope is to combine all that knowledge floating around into an understandable format for the reader.

Anton Swanepoel

Table of Contents

Anton Swanepoel

Anton Swanepoel

Chapter 1

What are deep stops?

Ask a tech diver if he/she believes in 'Deep Stops' and you may get a yes or no answer. However, ask the same diver what exactly deep stops are, and the answer may not be as clear. Even when the diver answers yes or no to believing in deep stops, you may then ask, which deep stops?

'Deep Stops' are actually many things. There are in fact many ways to calculate deep stops, with three methods currently being the most popular. So before we say that deep stops work or don't work, we have to be clear as to which one and what calculations for the stops we are talking about.

In essence, it is generally accepted that deep stops are stops done that are deeper than asked for by the decompression algorithm you use. However, herein lies the problem, for different algorithms could ask for different first stop depths. Your computer's algorithm for instance may require you to make the first stop at 70 ft, while your dive buddy's computer only asks for the first stop to be at 40 ft.

If you both stop at 70 ft for the first stop, your dive buddy is making a deep stop since the stop is deeper than required by his/her dive computer, while you are technically not making a deep stop for you are correctly following your computer's required stops.

Thus, decompression algorithms like VPM and RGBM that incorporate deeper stops than the normal Bühlmann algorithm are said to include deep stops, but if you follow the profile exactly then you are technically not making deep stops, for you are not incorporating deeper stops than the decompression algorithm asked for.

Anton Swanepoel

Due to this confusion where one algorithm's first scheduled stop may be another algorithm's deep stop it is now more common to say that deep stops are stops that are deeper than what the conventional Bühlmann algorithm would ask for.

However, even here is a problem, for one has to ask which Bühlmann algorithm and table, for he created many, and table ZHL17 incorporates group 0 with a two minute half time so as to create deeper stops than his previous models.

We see then that there are two classes of deep stops, each with two subclasses.

Empirical

In this class, deep stops are inserted manually or voluntarily (normally by the diver but could be from topside support or mission dive planners). This type of deep stop is one of the most widely practiced and will be discussed in more detail in later chapters.

-Subclass A

This stop is done on the fly underwater when the diver ascends and calculates the stop using the first scheduled stop that is displayed on the diver's decompression computer. The half your distance between your maximum depth and first required stop depth for two minutes is a classic example (Richard Pyle stop). If your dive buddy's computer asks for a deeper stop than your computer and you follow its profile, it falls into this category.

-Subclass B

Here the diver manually inserts a stop (or stops) before the dive into the dive profile. You may use the planning mode on your dive computer and compare it to your buddy's computer. If you note that your dive buddy's computer in planning mode requires a deeper stop than yours you can use it in the dive plan.

By noting the required deeper depth on a slate you now plan to stop at this depth. Additionally you may use the Richard Pyle method and calculate a stop deeper than your planning mode on your computer (laptop, smart phone or other device) requires. Additionally, you may use the planning feature on a computer program such as V-planner and note the stops it requires, then place them on a slate and execute those stops on the dive while then following your computer's recommendation for the shallow decompression part. The point is that the additional stops are pre-planned before the dive.

Model derived

The second class of deep stops are stops that a decompression algorithm or a manipulated decompression algorithm prescribed that are deeper than an unmanipulated model's first stop depth and are not ones the diver added to his/her profile.

-Subclass A

The first subclass is when divers using different decompression software programs or algorithms note different first stop depths. An overshadow from the empirical model can happen where a diver merges decompression profiles from a software program and his/her dive computer to make a new profile. Although this is almost the same as the empirical model, the difference is that the standard algorithm for the computer had to be modified (Gradient Factors or conservatism). Thus, you and your dive buddy can be using the same dive computer but your buddy selected a greater conservatism that now requires a deeper stop than your computer. Stops are then calculated or done on the fly as you ascend from the dive.

Anton Swanepoel

-Subclass B

In this subclass, stops are noted before the dive between different dive computers or possibly slates from software programs that have been modified to give greater conservatism. You can then before the dive note the differences and write a new plan on a slate to follow.

Thus even though the different stops may be from the same type of computer, the algorithm here needed to be adjusted to give a deeper stop and that deeper stop is planned into the dive profile before the dive is started.

Singing deep stop

Two old coral divers working in the 1950s relate how they used to stop at mid-depth on ascent from a deep dive to sing a gospel. They would adapt the number of verses they sang according to how comfortable they felt with the decompression. One can learn interesting things from old timers, even if at the time it made no sense, now we know they knew things many so-called experts ignored. This would then add another way of calculating deep stops, stop at half the depth and sing some songs. ☺

Note on inserting deep stops

Divers may insert deep stops due to the diver believing it will make the dive safer or due to the diver believing doing so may make the shallow decompression shorter. Sometimes divers may insert deep stops with the belief that the stops will make the dive safer and shorter. However, standard Bühlmann algorithm dive computers will normally require longer shallow stops if you insert an additional deep stop, and some dual phase bubble model dive computers may give you credit for stopping deeper and require fewer shallow decompression stops and times regardless of your beliefs. Thus if your computer reduces the shallow stops and you want to stay with the original long shallow decompression, you may need to calculate that yourself.

Deep stop definition

Deep stops are then any stops that are done that are deeper than standard Haldanian models would ask for. The stops can be manually calculated by the diver during or before the dive and can be from any manual calculation method or due to an altered algorithm (Gradient Factors or changing conservatism), or an algorithm that by itself requires deeper stops than standard Haldanian models (such as bubble models).

Anton Swanepoel

Chapter 2

Deep stop origin

The concept of stopping deeper or 'Deep Stops' is not a relatively new idea, Paul Bert was the first to introduce the concept of deep stops when he suggested a stop at 15 m (around 50 ft) for 15 minutes to hard hat divers that dove to 30 m (around 99 ft) at the time. He published his ideas in a book called '*La Pression Barometrique*', 1878.

Haldane also noted that ascending up to half the atmospheric pressure (such as 4 to 2 ata) seemed safe and did theorize that deeper stops or a reduced pressure gradient may be required for deep dives. However, deep stops were not introduced in deco tables, but rather long shallow stops near the surface. Haldane did not think it was needed to include a deeper stop in his tables for he believed that divers ascending from 100 ft would have any bubbles crushed by the pressure.

A tissue compartment 0 (tissue half time 2 minutes) was later added to the Bühlmann algorithm ZH-L16 as the 17th tissue (model ZH-L17B$_{TS}$) to create deeper first stops when using the Bühlmann tables.

Physicist David Yount (professor of physics at the University of Hawaii) did research on bubble formation in the 1950s and focused on the first stop where bubbles are more likely to form. Although he had good results from his initial trials, divers were so stuck to conventional profiles that his idea of spending time deeper was heavily resisted. Yount's work later became the basis for several theories, including VPM and RGBM.

Deep stops were later investigated by Dr. Richard L. Pyle (credited for raising awareness of deeper stops). Dr. Pyle used to do many dives in the 180 to 220 ft range to collect fish specimens, and noted that on some dives he was fine after a dive while on others he had varied symptoms (mild to extreme tiredness and tingling to name a few).

Dr. Pyle began to monitor the symptoms and noted his dive profiles to find a correlation. He realized that on dives that he did not collect fish, he felt worse. After some thought he realized that on his dives (mostly 200 ft) he made a 2 to 3 minute stop at around 125 ft when he caught some fish, that he did not execute when he had no fish.

Since most fish have a swim bladder to control their buoyancy, Dr. Pyle had to stop at depth to insert a hypodermic needle into the fishes' swim bladder in order to release the gas, else the swim bladder will expand, crushing the internal organs, causing death.

Since Dr. Pyle's first decompression scheduled stop was normally around 50 ft, the 125 ft stop of around 2 to 3 minutes to treat the fish was nicely in the middle between his bottom depth and the first deco stop. Dr. Pyle then started to include this stop in all his dives, whether he caught fish or not, and the results were no symptoms of tiredness.

When Dr. Pyle brought his ideas to the diving community, it was not accepted by many 'experts', resulting in Pyle continuing alone until 1989 when he met Dr. David Yount at an American Academy of Underwater Sciences (AAUS) meeting. Dr Yount is one of the creators of the Varying-Permeability Model (VPM). Yount's ideas made sense to Pyle as he had hard proof that stopping deeper had a positive effect on his dive.

VPM was first introduced in 1986 and was completed in 2000. 2002 saw the bubble tracing logic added (VPM-B) and 2005 saw the extreme calculations logic added (VPM-B/E). VPM-B/E was originally designed for Dave Shaw's second 270 m (886 ft) dive that was scheduled to take place in the Boesmansgat cave, South Africa, but is now widely used. The E variation logic only employs the extreme calculations on longer dives (normally dives longer than 90 minutes) and adds additional conservatism.

2011 saw the introduction of VPM-B/GFS by Shearwater (Gradient Factor Surfacing) and Asser Salama introduced the VPM-B/U (Ultimate). All variations from the VPM-B model (E, U and GFS variants) aim to generate a more conservative schedule.

VPM models incorporate deeper stops than normally called for by compartment or tissue loading (such as Bühlmann or Haldanian) models. Pyle expanded on these theories in combination with his own experience of making deeper stops and created what is now known as the Pyle stop (stop at half the distance between your maximum depth and first deco stop).

In 1992 Dr. Bruce Wienke started writing about diving topics and included decompression theories in controlling the bubble volume rather than letting it grow and trying to treat it later with long decompression stops. He started working on a reduced gradient bubble model (RGBM).

In 1997 Dr. Wienke agreed to help NAUI with developing dive tables based on his RGBM model. The RGBM model would later form the basis for many dive computers and dive tables.

Chapter 3

Role of safety stops in recreational diving

A safety stop at around 15 to 20 ft for around 3 to 5 minutes is today taught by many dive certification agencies. People know they need to make a safety stop, but many have no idea why.

Protecting the brain

Safety stops in recreational diving are all to do with bubbles and fast tissues, while adding some safety buffer as a cherry on the cake. Original DCS incidences in recreational divers were more towards neurological hits than pain only. At the time the 60 ft/minute ascent rate that was established in 1956 by the Navy was used. However when the ascent speed was selected it was not for no stop dives and divers did not ascend directly to the surface, but stopped at pre planned depths to do decompression.

When the ascent rate was lowered in recreational diving to 30 ft/minute, the incidence of neurological DCS dropped dramatically, however it was still high and investigations revealed that divers were still not slowing down correctly on the ascent (hard to do with the dive gear at the time as few had dive computers). Many divers also only paid lip service to the slow ascent recommendation, thus it was then decided to implement a safety stop. It was noted that a dive with an ascent speed of 30 ft/minute with no stop had around the same effect on bubble scores as a dive with a stop at 15 ft for 3 minutes using an ascent speed of 60 ft/minute.

Note, for no decompression dives a too slow ascent is also not recommended, thus an ascent slower than 25 ft/minute is not recommended.

Anton Swanepoel

Thus doing a safety stop helps to prevent bubbles from forming in the fast tissues (especially the brain and spinal column) and prevent neurological DCS.

10, 15 or 20 ft safety stop?

Although a stop at 15 ft was introduced, 20 ft was initially selected as this was the depth where critical supersaturation mostly occurred in recreational divers for the profiles that were dove at the time, although 10 ft was also suggested as many tech divers did their last decompression stop at 10 ft. 15 ft was the middle ground and selected.

Currently most people make a stop at around 15 ft, however many computers start the safety stop countdown from 19 or 20 ft. A 3 minute stop at 20 ft followed by a 3 minute stop at 15 ft is more ideal. This follows from a study done for safety stops at different depths. Two groups did exactly the same dive profile in bottom time and depth, but one group made a 5 minute stop at 10 ft and the second group a 1 minute stop at 20 ft followed by a 4 minute stop at 10 ft. The group with the 1 minute stop at 20 ft had significantly lower bubble scores not only upon surfacing, but also hours after the dive.

Tests have shown that the US Navy "no-decompression" limits do produce bubble nuclei in all subjects after dives and in most cases is not conservative enough for non military divers. However, in Navy tests it was found that including a stop of around 1 to 2 minutes at 20 ft almost eliminated bubbles after a dive.

From a paper presented by Donald R. Short from the College of Sciences, San Diego State University at the 1989 Biomechanics of safe ascents workshop, it is noted in calculations that a safety stop for 3 minutes at 20 ft should be done on all dives, especially those below 60 ft.

It was calculated that there was only a slight improvement between a 5 and a 3 minute stop, but that there was a marked improvement between doing the stop at 20 ft compared to 15 ft with 20 ft being better.

More and more people are now realizing that stopping earlier (20 ft) is seen to be safer and incorporate this into their dive plan. One wonders if this is not the same principle as 'Deep Stops'.

Extra safety

Safety stops also give an additional safety buffer as a bonus. If you exceed the time limit that your body would have coped with a direct ascent (even if within table limits), then the safety stop may help to off-gas the excess gas enough to prevent a DCS hit, or reduce the severity of the hit. Remember tables are not 100% safe for all people all the time.

In 1958 the French naval Groupe d'Etudes et de Recherches Sous-Marines de la Marine Nationale (GERS) published a book called La Plongée (many members were associated with Cousteau). The book suggested a max no decompression depth of 40 m (132 ft) for 15 min. It was stated that divers should take at least one minute to ascend the last 10 m (33 ft/minute ascent) and on dives deeper than 40 m a stop at 3 m (around 10 ft) must be made, failing this tended to result in illness.

Affect of safety stops on different bottom depths

Safety stops have been seen to make a marked improvement in bubble scores on deeper dives (recreational), especially ones deeper than 100 ft, and is due to the fast tissues off-gassing on ascent creating a large pressure difference and controlling the dive. However, on shallower dives (60 ft and less) the improvement of making a safety stop is not the same as for a deep dive due to the slower compartments now starting to control the dive.

Anton Swanepoel

Looking at it mathematically, for a dive to 110 ft for 20 minutes, the 10 minute compartment normally controls the dive, and on a dive to 70 ft for 50 minutes, the 40 minute compartment normally controls the dive (depending on the algorithm used). Thus a five minute safety stop will allow the 10 minute compartment to reduce its gas pressure by 25%, where the 40 minute compartment will only reduce its pressure by 6.25%. Thus safety stops become more and more important the deeper the dive, however it is still an improvement to just coming straight to the surface without stopping on a shallow dive.

Conclusion

Safety stops are more to slow down the ascent speed and prevent divers from making a fast direct ascent from depth to the surface. However, should the diver make a slow ascent, then the 3 or 5 minute safety stop time gives added safety against DCS.

The advice is then for recreational divers to keep an eye on their ascent speed (many computers will sound an alarm if you exceed 30 ft/minute) and make a safety stop. For multilevel dives the safety stop does not have as much an effect as a square profile dive but still makes a difference.

Deep stop and safety stop

If you did a square profile, then a 2 ½ minute stop at half the max depth is sometimes advised in addition to the safety stop, normally when following a 60 ft/minute ascent rate. (Although the deep stop is not accepted by all as more tests and proof is asked for by some to prove the effectiveness in recreational diving of including a deep stop.) Should you wish to add the deep stop, count it as part of your bottom time (time spent at your maximum depth). Thus the total bottom time you dove for plus the deep stop time together must not exceed the no decompression limits of your tables or computer used.

Note on the last 15 ft

Although divers are becoming more aware of the need for a slow ascent and a safety stop, some divers do not realize that the ascent speed from the safety stop to the surface is also important.

Some divers fully inflate their buoyancy compensator / control device (BCD) after they completed their safety stop and pop to the surface. In tests done it was found that doing this, the rate of ascent can exceed 250 ft/minute. Since the last 30 ft has the greatest pressure change, this can result in problems. It is advised to slow down the last ascent from your safety stop to around 15 ft/minute or slower.

From 15 ft to the surface, the pressure drops around 50%, thus any bubbles already in the system have the potential of growing by around 50% in size and it is possible for nuclei to form bubbles due to a sudden reduction in ambient pressure (on a fast ascent gas may diffuse out of the fast tissues into a bubble and actual bubble size increase may be 100%).

If a slow ascent is done, it helps the faster tissues to off-gas and helps prevent bubbles from forming in nuclei. Any existing bubbles may be prevented from enlarging (dissolved gas from a tissue may enter a bubble already formed in or close to the tissues instead of the blood).

What is the rush anyway, do you need to rush up to get a beer or rush up to go to the recompression chamber? ☺

The 500 psi reserve rule

Many instructors teach divers to finish their dive with at least 500 psi in their tanks at the end of the dive when they surface, some ask nicely while others scream at their students (and even customers) for not ending the dive with this reserve. So let's look at this a bit more objectively.

Firstly, yes you do want some pressure in your tank left when you surface for a number of reasons. It makes it easier to inflate your BCD using the power inflator, and since a great deal of panics and problems occur on the surface it is logical to want to have the diver float with ease.

In addition, you want to prevent water from entering your tank, however there is a very small chance of this happening with modern scuba gear even if you breathe your tank down until there is nothing (never recommended, purely noted for academic purpose). The first stage needs an amount (normally 5 to 10 bar, 150 psi) of pressure in the tank more than ambient pressure to function, thus there will still be pressure in the tank even if your regulator says ..... nothing.

A reserve is also needed should you or your buddy accidentally exceed your allowable bottom time and need to make an emergency decompression stop (recreational diving). Alternatively, if you need to assist your buddy, who is low or out of air at the bottom, then having that additional amount of gas will normally allow you to bring both of you to the surface.

What can be done with the extra gas?

Now, just imagine all went well, you had a nice dive and did your safety stop (3 to 5 minutes) and have 500 psi left in your tank, you are directly under the boat (or by the exit) and it is a calm day. For an average resting diver, 0.6 cu ft/minute air consumption is not unreasonable, thus you will be using around 33 psi/minute at 15 ft out of a normal 80 cu ft tank. With this consumption, you can possibly make an additional 3 minute safety stop and need only 100 psi, leaving you 400 psi spare.

An additional 3 minute stop will especially serve you well if you did a deep dive.

Is it in this case not safer (lower DCS risk) to come up at 400 psi than 500 psi? This you need to answer for yourself, but consider this, what is the difference between 400 or even 100 psi and 500 psi when you are done with your dive? (*Note, not advocating finishing the dive with less than 500 psi, it is better to plan that extra safety stop into your gas consumption if you want to do it, but if you end the dive and are still at your safety stop and have that nagging feeling that maybe an additional 3 or 5 minutes at 15 ft is a good idea, it is normally a good idea to listen to that small voice inside, ask any tech diver*).

Chapter 4

The role of deep stops in diving

So what is the actual fuss then all about, and why bother to incorporate deep stops or deeper stops in a dive profile then?

Considering the different algorithms and thoughts on why DCS happens, this can become a very interesting and deep discussion, however the bottom line still is in its simplest form; to reduce the risk of DCS. Deep stops then have the same purpose in general as safety stops, to reduce DCS risk (see previous chapter if not already done so).

Link between venous bubbles and DCS

Although the exact cause of DCS including the link between venous gas emboli (VGE), dehydration and micro bubbles are not known, it is theorized that bubbles play a critical role in DCS. If bubble formation can be prevented or limited then DCS risk can possibly be reduced. In a study with 1726 air dives and 1508 heliox dives, an extremely poor relation between bubble scores and predicting positive DCS was found, however a very strong link between no bubbles or very low bubble scores and predicting no DCS was found.

Supersaturation

It is known that supersaturation is needed for bubbles to form, thus if the pressure ratio difference between inert gas in tissues and the inspired inert gas is reduced on ascent, then it might be possible to stop bubbles from forming as the pressure difference will be below the trigger point. The reason it is seen to stop deeper for a short time is to allow the faster tissues to off-gas before bubbles form. As noted from the previous chapter, these tissues affect the brain and spinal column greatly (the spinal cord is around 12 ½ minute half time).

How to reduce supersaturation

Supersaturation levels can be reduced in two ways on ascent, by either slowing the ascent down to give the tissues time to off-gas sufficiently (at the cost of additional gas on-gassing for slower tissues that need additional decompression time), or by incorporating stops (staircase or staged ascent).

-Slow bleed ascent

Saturation divers normally use a slow ascent where tech divers normally use a staged ascent. A slow bleed ascent was actually first introduced by Sir Leonard Hill. See chapter on ascent speed for more information.

-Staged ascent

The staged ascent is calculated to incorporate a stop each time a tissue inert gas would exceed a pressure difference against ambient pressure that is seen to have a high risk in triggering bubbles to form (where any compartment reaches a critical supersaturation level). See chapter on ascent speed for more information.

Supersaturation levels between compartments

Initially it was thought that fast compartments could handle a high supersaturation value. However from the neurological DCS incidence cases in recreational diving it was noted that this may not always be the case. Incorporating deeper short stops may then help to reduce supersaturation levels in the fast compartments and reduce neurological DCS incidences.

Conclusion

Deep stops then serve very much the same role as safety stops, to slow down ascent speed and reduce DCS risk, especially CNS DCS by preventing bubbles from forming or growing. As seen from safety stops, deeper has its merits (problem is how deep).

Anton Swanepoel

Chapter 5

How long to stop for

Just to make the whole deep stop argument even more interesting, there is also the question of how long do you stop for? Some say 1 minute stops, most say 2 minutes while others go as high as 5 minutes. There is also a thought about not doing an actual stop, but to rather slow the ascent down to around 10 to 15 ft/minute and even as slow as 5 ft/minute (normally when approaching any stop depth).

1 minute slow ascent

The basic thinking is that one wants to slow the ascent in order to help prevent bubbles from forming and any bubbles that are already there from enlarging beyond a critical volume. If the ascent is slowed, the dissolved gas has time to exit the tissues without bubbles forming and bubbles already in the system have time to dissolve or shrink before they are too large to cause any problems.

There are two main stop size ranges used, 10 and 15 ft. Thus one would make an ascent of one minute between the stop sizes. If one chooses 10 ft, then one would do 10 ft/minute on ascent, and 15 ft/minute if you were to choose a 15 ft stop size. The actual distance then becomes a moving stop, sometimes seen in desktop dive planners such as V-planner where a 1 minute stop will be given for every 10 ft increment for certain sections of the ascent.

The risk however is that slower tissues may on-gas and lengthen shallow decompression stops. From tests done, slower ascent (10 ft/minute) resulted in more bubbles detected after the dive than faster ascents (30 ft/minute).

1 minute stop

From tests done by Divers Alert Network (DAN) International on recreational diving it was shown that a 1 minute deep stop was not adequate for recreational divers. It is also noted from tests on decompression dives that a 1 minute deep stop is not enough time to give the fast compartments time to off-gas.

1 – 2 combination

A one–two combination is when one does a 1 minute deep stop at half the depth and a 2 minute safety stop. From the DAN International research on recreational diving this has been shown to be only marginally better than making no stops at all.

2 ½ minute stops

Two ½ minute stops seemed to work the best from tests done and is now incorporated in the NAUI hard tables (recreational diving). The two to two ½ minute stops are also mostly used by tech divers as it gives the two and four minute compartments enough time to off-gas. 50% for the two minute and 25% reduction for the four minute compartment in supersaturation values.

Longer than 2 ½ minutes

Deep stops longer than two ½ minutes did not seem to improve bubble scores and may in fact create more bubbles on certain dives. DAN International's tests and later tests by NAUI favored two ½ minute stops. However, this is for recreational diving and different profiles may require different stops, longer decompression profiles may require longer stops. However, even in deep tech diving (not saturation diving) doing longer than two ½ minute stops for the initial stops is seen as too long. Later decompression stops may become longer as slower tissues reach critical supersaturation.

Anton Swanepoel

Extending 20 and 30 ft stops

In tunnel workers doing extended periods of work under pressure, numerous tests have been done to shorten their decompression obligation. In tests by Hill (released in Feb 1970) it was found that overall decompression can be shortened if the stops at 20 and 30 ft stops were lengthened compared to ascending sooner to the 10 ft stop. Behnke (1941) and Kindwall (undersea medical research December 1975) showed that more gas can be eliminated at deeper (50 ft) than at 10 ft for the same amount of time.

For recreational diving, if you are within the no decompression limits, then making a 1 to 2 minute stop at 30 ft followed by a 3 minute stop at 20 ft will greatly lower bubble scores, especially for deep bounce dives.

For decompression diving, adding an additional two to five minutes to the 30 ft stop and three to six minutes to the 20 ft stop, in addition to making the last stop at 15 ft instead of 10 ft, may depending on the dive and deco gas breathed, substantially lower bubble scores on surfacing.

Conclusion

From current tests and understanding of decompression, it seems that two ½ minutes give the best overall results on deep stops. However, most tests were for square profiles and any multilevel diving could possibly invalidate this time and possibly deep stops altogether as the multilevel could be seen as extended stops at different levels, especially for shallow dives (60 ft and shallower).

Chapter 6

Tests done for deep stops

Following is a summary of a collection of tests done by various agencies and their results on deep stops.

US Navy, 1970s

The US Navy conducted tests on divers in the middle of the 1970s to test for the reliability of Doppler bubble scores, however interesting discoveries were made in relation to deeper stops than asked for by the schedule. The schedule used was a 210 ft dive on air for 50 minutes (a then untested schedule) and a 132 ft dive for 30 minutes. These were all dry chamber dives.

A deep stop was made for three minutes at 10 ft deeper than the original schedule (70 ft compared to 60 ft) with the control group making the first stop at 60 ft and the rest of the decompression being the same for both. An additional group used a longer decompression schedule (220 ft for 50 minute table), although their first stop was also 60 ft as the control with just more shallow deco.

From the results, the group doing the additional three minute deep stop had lower bubble scores than both the control and additional decompression group. The control and additional decompression group had no significant difference in bubble scores between them; however no divers in either the deep stop group or the additional deco group had DCS, while divers in the original schedule group did get DCS.

For the 132 ft test, an additional two minute stop was added 10 ft deeper than the control group (40 ft compared to 30 ft), while the remaining decompression was the same. The results were the same as the 210 ft dive; the group doing the extra deep stop had significant lower bubble scores than the control group.

Anton Swanepoel

From the results it can be seen that small changes in decompression schedules can have a significant effect on bubble scores after a dive (another reason to keep ascent speeds and depth control at decompression stops correct). Even though the results seem to favor deep stops, it should be noted that only one stop was inserted and only 10 ft deeper than the first required decompression stop, in addition to the test being done on air bottom gas and air deco in a dry chamber. If the same results will be seen on tri-mix, higher oxygen content decompression gas, deeper or more stops needs additional testing.

LANL databank

The LANL databank is a collection of dive profiles from various sources that includes individual technical divers. Divers using the profile are asked to report their dive profile data to the bank. Data includes ascent and descent rates, bottom gas, maximum depth, total dive time and diver personal details such as age, weight and sex. (Not yes or no. ☺)

The databank data is then used to create a bubble model (RGBM) that is used in various applications and forms the basis for many tables and computers, such as NAUI RGBM tables, ANDI, Mares, Suunto, Dacor, GAP, ABYSS and Hydrospace, to name a few.

Being a bubble model the algorithm uses a phase volume constraint in the dive profile to track bubbles. This algorithm then estimates the volume and number of bubbles and tries to keep the amount and size of the bubbles below a value calculated to be safe to surface with.

In 2008 the databank had just below 3000 profiles from 150 ft to 840 ft with 20 cases of DCS.

However, an estimated over two million dives have been done using either RGBM tables or computers employing the algorithm in recreational diving with few reported cases of DCS compared to the dives done. An additional over 20 000 technical dives with few DCS cases were also done.

From the sheer amount of dives done on this model (RGBM) it would seem to favor deep stops. However it should be noted that there is little actual tests or control groups. Many of the dives are recreational or training dives that are in many cases far below already established reasonable safe table times (60 ft for 55 minutes).

Further it should be noted that these tables and computers are very conservative. Reducing bottom time or lengthening decompression time lowers DCS risk (see US Navy test done) without lowering bubble scores. The fact that most of these dives have no bubble scores recorded and no controls to test against makes them objective, as both the longer deco time and deep stop groups from the US Navy test did not get DCS.

It should also be noted that even though many divers dive with these tables and computers, many recreational divers do not employ a deep stop in recreational profiles and even for decompression, as many divers (author included) do not activate the RGBM featured deep stops on the computer, thus those dives cannot be counted towards deep stop successes.

The deep stop function not being activated in itself leans towards that not making deep stops also works when the available bottom time is shortened or decompression lengthened.
(*Author's note, the deep stop feature not activated by the author is due to the computer used by the author (Suunto D6) mainly being used for recreational training dives and in many cases it is impossible to make the suggested deep stops while running a recreational class, and not because the author does not believe in the validity of deep stops*).

It should also be noted that many users do not use the deep stop function as they have no knowledge that it exists or how to use it. This is seen from over seven years of teaching and guiding divers, where many divers have in fact only a limited knowledge about decompression and decompression stops, leading the author to write 'Dive Computers' to help divers know more about dive computers and how to use them.
www.antonswanepoelbooks.com/dive_computers.php

It should furthermore be noted that not all divers report symptoms that, had it been reported, would have led to treatment for DCS. In a study done in around 1998, it was found that up to 70% of experienced divers have had symptoms that if reported would have led to treatment for DCS. If they actually had DCS that resolved over time or if it was something else is not known.

Woodville Karst Plain Project (WKPP)

In the late 1980s a group of divers started experimenting with deep cave dives. The divers extended their dives while focusing on safety and by the mid 1990s were already doing dives to 300 ft with six hours bottom time. After 20 years of diving and around 7500 dives they are doing dives with up to 10 hours bottom time (17 hours deco incurred) with most dives around 280 ft and six hours bottom time.

Due to the experiments done by the divers, they slowly started making deeper stops than called for by Bühlmann tables and shorter decompression times. Time as much as 300 minutes less decompression compared to Bühlmann tables are recorded.

From this data it would seem deep stops and shorter decompression works. However, it should be noted that there are only a limited number of divers using these profiles and that there is no documented control to compare dives with each other in regard to scientific validity.

It should also be noted that Helium diffusion rates according to Bühlmann tables are seen as incorrect, leading to longer decompression suggestions on dives using Helium in the breathing mix than what is actually needed most of the time.

The end thought from these dives however is that dives thought to be unconventional may work and that what we think we know is not always correct or the best correct answer.

ANDI tests

American Nitrox Divers International (ANDI) started doing tests in 1990 for CCR software. In the early models the software incorporated deep stops and asked for a two minute stop when 50% of the maximum depth was reached on ascent. The decompression schedule seemed correct as no DCS hits were recorded. In 2003 ANDI incorporated RGBM into their dive planner, called 'ANDI dive planner', later to become 'ANDI-GAP'. ANDI trained commercial divers in 2003 for the Rio-Antirion bridge project with great results. In 2004 ANDI trained the Israeli army, Navy and IDF. In over 1000 documented dives to between 60 and 103 meters (200 and 340 ft) no incidence of DCS was recorded.

ANDI has recorded more successes and decided to implement the ANDI-GAP tables and software in all ANDI technical training. With a recorded over 16 000 divers using the ANDI-GAP software it is an impressive record. However, as with the RGBM and VPM models, having no actual tests with controls and recorded bubble score counts it is hard to say if the model is better than other models. As noted from the US Navy test, bubble scores can be higher without divers getting DCS.

Anton Swanepoel

NEDU tests between bubble and tissue loading model

The Navy Experimental Diving Unit (NEDU) did tests to compare tissue loading models to bubble models that employ deeper stops.

A wet chamber was used for the tests, and divers were taken to 170 ft at a descent rate of 60 ft/minute. Bottom time was 30 minutes where an exact amount of work was done (115 watt cycle Ergometer). Ascent speed was 30 ft/minute with a 174 minute decompression time. Decompression time was the same, but the stop depths were different for each algorithm with the bubble model having stops start deeper.

Although 375 man-dives on each schedule were planned, the test was stopped after 390 dives were done by 81 divers. At this point (mid point) 11 cases of DCS were already recorded on the bubble model compared to only three on the tissue loading model.

It was also recorded that venous gas emboli (VGE) scores were significantly higher for the bubble model dives compared to the tissue loading model.

It was concluded from the test that inserting deeper stops just below the first prescribed decompression depth can be beneficial in certain circumstances, however it does not shorten decompression but actually addresses a shortcoming in the original schedule and that decompression should be increased. However, inserting more and or deeper stops may in fact slow down the gas elimination and possibly cause additional gas uptake that will need additional decompression, leading to increased risk of DCS and higher VGE scores after a dive.

French Navy tests

The French navy uses the MN90 (MN= Marine Nationale) deep air table for air dives to 60 m (200 ft) and the MN78 for tri-mix diving to 80 m (264 ft). The combined incidence rate is one in 30 000 (however the deep air alone incidence is one in 3000). With 89% of the DCS cases reported being neurological related, it was suggested that incorporating deep stops to account for faster tissue supersaturation (five to 30 minute half times) would lower the DCS incidence and especially the neurological incidence (tables are Haldanian based with 20 compartments).

A total of six ascent profiles was tested using 12 navy divers with deep stops for air added at ½ the absolute depth and for tri-mix at 1/3 the absolute depth, all dives were done in a wet chamber. Bubble tests were done at a 30 minute interval for between two to five hours depending on the profile, using both continuous Doppler 5Mhz and a pulse Doppler 2Mhz.

From the tests the standard tables (MN90 and MN78) did not produce significant differences in bubble scores compared to most of the deep stop profiles run. However in a comparison with a slowed ascent profile that incorporated deep stops and reduced decompression time (as normally advocated one can do on bubble models) there was an increased level of prolonged bubbling that was noted in all divers that did the profile (eight) and tiredness in five of the divers.

In the deep air diving profiles it was found that incorporating additional stops that lengthen ascent time actually increased bubbling, and incorporating only one two minute deep stop had no effect. For air, adding deep stops could reduce bubble formation in faster compartments (brain and spinal column), but deep stops do not always reduce decompression stress (total number of bubbles).

Anton Swanepoel

For the tri-mix dives following the results it seems safer to breathe oxygen at the shallow stops than incorporate deep stops.

For both air and tri-mix the conclusion was that deep stops are not proven beneficial for deep air diving to 60 m (200 ft) and for bounce dives to 100 m (330 ft) on tri-mix, and instead increasing the inspired oxygen on decompression may be more beneficial.

Conclusion

As can be seen, deep stops do in some cases reduce bubble scores and reduce DCS risk, while in other cases it may increase bubble scores. It is due to this conflict between tests that when and how to do deep stops is unclear. For yes it can reduce DCS risk if done correctly, but due to the increased DCS risk if done incorrectly, in addition to not knowing when a deep stop is correct and when it is incorrect, has led many divers to elect rather to stay with what they know has been tested until more testing on deep stops is done.

When testing and further understanding of bubbles and decompression gets us to the point when we can say this is the guideline for how deep to stop for how long, 'Deep Stops' may be the thing of the past since you would not need to alter your computer's dive profile. For then the new knowledge will be incorporated into new tables and dive computers and the algorithms will automatically ask for these stops. Deep stops would then be a thing of 'How we used to do it before we knew better.'

Chapter 7

Risk of adding too many stops

One may assume that slowing the ascent or adding additional stops will prevent or limit bubble growth and reduce DCS risk; however, what is the drawback of adding too many or too deep stops? It has to be remembered that a deep stop in this case is a stop deeper than prescribed by the algorithm used.

Safe ascent depth

The safe ascent depth (SAD) is the shallowest depth you can ascend to according to the algorithm used and is controlled by any tissue compartment that reaches its maximum supersaturation pressure, called the controlling compartment.

If the new or deeper stop that is added is deeper than the SAD, then that compartment and all faster compartments will continue to off-gas at the deeper stop and the pressure gradient for those compartments will be lower when you reach the original SAD. However, any slower compartments that have an inert gas pressure lower than the inserted deep stop ambient pressure will continue to on-gas. Those compartments might then require additional decompression time on shallower stops to off-gas the additional dissolved gas acquired at the deep stop. This partly explains the higher DCS incidences on some tests where inserting deep stops increased bubble scores and DCS risk.

The same effect can actually be reached by slowing the ascent rate (partly the idea behind the five to 15 ft/minute ascent speed) and may actually just fix a flaw in the original schedule.

If not many stops are added or the ascent hasn't slowed too much from the original schedule, one could possibly get away with not doing the additional decompression required without increasing the DCS risk notably.

Anton Swanepoel

If the original schedule was flawed and allowed bubbles to form, then the added stops may actually prevent or lessen the amount of bubbles that form on the ascent. This will enhance the shallow decompression times and subsequently show as lower bubble scores after the dive, in addition to partly explaining why some tests show better results for inserting a deep stop.

For example:
Let's assume that on a dive to 200 ft for a given time the optimum first stop is 125 ft. If the original dive schedule asked for the first stop to be at 25 ft, then the pull from max depth to the first stop is extremely large and also very far from the optimal stop. If one were to now add a deep stop, let's say using a Pyle stop, then we would end up with: 200 – 25 = 175 / 2 = 87.5 + 25 = 112.5 ft. So although this stop is not at the optimal stop depth, it is far closer and will enhance the safety of the dive in addition to possibly preventing bubbles from forming, enhancing the efficiency of the shallow deco. One may even be able to cut the shallow deco shorter in this instance.

However, what if the first stop was at 80 ft? In this case the pull is not as large, even though the first stop is still not at the optimal first stop depth. If we do the same calculations for adding a deeper deep stop we end up with: 200 – 80 = 120 / 2 = 60 + 80 = 140 ft. Thus our new deep stop will be at 140 ft, however this is deeper than the optimal first stop and although it may stop bubbles from forming, it may now allow slower tissues to on-gas additional inert gas that needs to be eliminated at the shallow stops. If the shallow stops are not increased, this deeper stop may actually cause more harm than good (seen in some cases where adding a deeper stop resulted in a higher DCS incidence and a higher bubble score).

If the original first stop was at 50 ft, then the calculations would have resulted in a new deep stop of 125 ft, the optimal stop for this profile.

We note then that the effect a deeper deep stop has on the dive is linked to how far the original first stop was from the optimal first stop for that exact dive profile (depth, bottom time, ascent and descent speed) and how far the new deep stop is away from the optimal first stop depth.

New SAD

It is also possible for a slower compartment to on-gas so much that it now becomes the controlling compartment and its SAD may be deeper than the original first stop. If you were to now ascend to the original first stop after making a manually inserted deep stop you may exceed the critical supersaturation in this tissue and possibly trigger bubbles to form.

Conclusion

As can be seen, the value and effect a deep stop has on a profile is largely dependent on not only the ascent speed of the original profile, but also the new ascent speed and the validity of the original profile. The more correct the original profile was, the less effect a deep stop will have, the more the profile was flawed, the greater effect the deep stop will have (either good or bad, if the original decompression was too short to start with, adding deep stops may increase its shortcomings).

Chapter 8

Diffusion speed and solubility

In order to understand on- and off-gassing between different inert gasses, it is important that one first understands the difference between the diffusion speed of a gas and its solubility in a tissue.

Diffusion speed

Diffusion speed (often just called diffusion) is how fast a molecule of a given gas will enter a tissue. The rate is dependent upon many factors such as the mass of the molecules, the ambient temperature, ambient pressure, the fraction of the gas (partial pressure), and the tissue type. Basically, how badly it wants to get in or out.

Solubility

The solubility of a gas is how much gas will dissolve into a given tissue, or how greedy the gas is for space. A tissue will absorb a larger volume of a highly soluble gas compared to a lower solubility gas before reaching any given partial pressure. Thus, a greater volume of a highly soluble gas needs to dissolve into a tissue to reach the same partial pressure as a lower solubility gas.

Gas behavior in a liquid

The first thing we need to realize is that gas dissolved in a liquid does not exert hydrostatic pressure as it would in a gas phase where the gas molecules are free to move around. Thus what we call the partial pressure of a gas dissolved in a liquid is the partial pressure that the gas would exert if the gas phase were in equilibrium with the liquid and is an index of the amount of gas currently dissolved in the tissue.

For example, if a tissue has a partial pressure of 1 ata nitrogen and 1 ata helium, then there will be more nitrogen in the tissue as nitrogen is more soluble than helium.

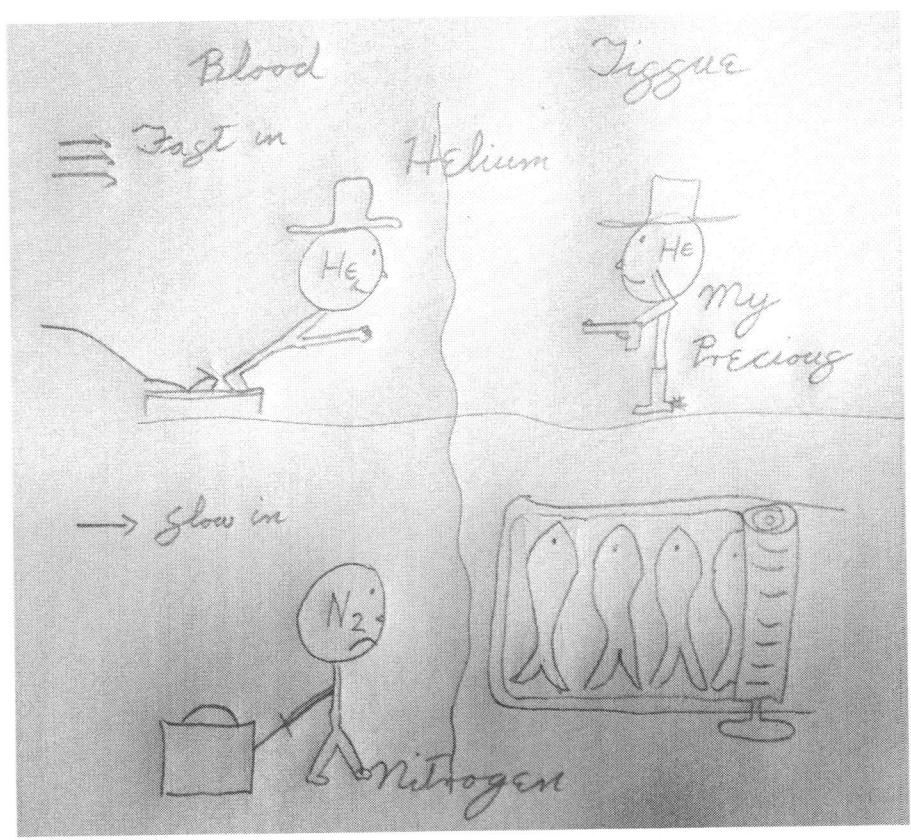

A cartoon drawing by the author showing the relationship between solubility and diffusion speed for nitrogen and helium. Helium is more eager to enter or diffuse into a tissue than nitrogen, however helium is a greedy gas and does not like to share as much space. Nitrogen on the other hand, although slower to enter than helium, is far more willing to share the same space with other nitrogen molecules. Thus, a greater volume of nitrogen will occupy and create the same pressure when compared to the same helium pressure.

Anton Swanepoel

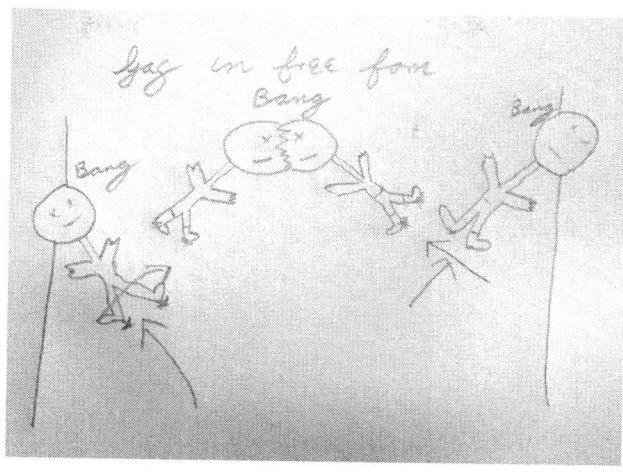

Gas in free form exerting pressure on the container wall and on other gas molecules in the mix, if the temperature is raised then the pressure will increase (if the container does not increase in size).

In solution the gas molecules are not as free to move around and thus will exert very little pressure on its surroundings or other molecules.

Gas movement

Gas molecules move all the time when in a gas phase, even if it is in an equilibrium state with ambient pressure. In equilibrium, the gas dissolving into a tissue is the same volume as the gas diffusing out of the tissue thus the partial pressure in the tissue stays constant. If the pressure differs, then gas will diffuse from an area of higher partial pressure to an area of lower partial pressure.

Note that diffusion of a gas is not a bulk movement of gas but the movement of individual gas molecules. Thus the diffusion of a gas in or out of a tissue is dependent only on the partial pressure gradient of the gas dissolved in the tissue and that outside the tissue of the same gas and not on other gases present in the tissue, each gas for himself basically. Different dissolved gasses also do not act on each other in the tissue, thus one will not push the other out. If one gas is removed from a tissue the other gases will not expand to fill the vacated partial pressure.

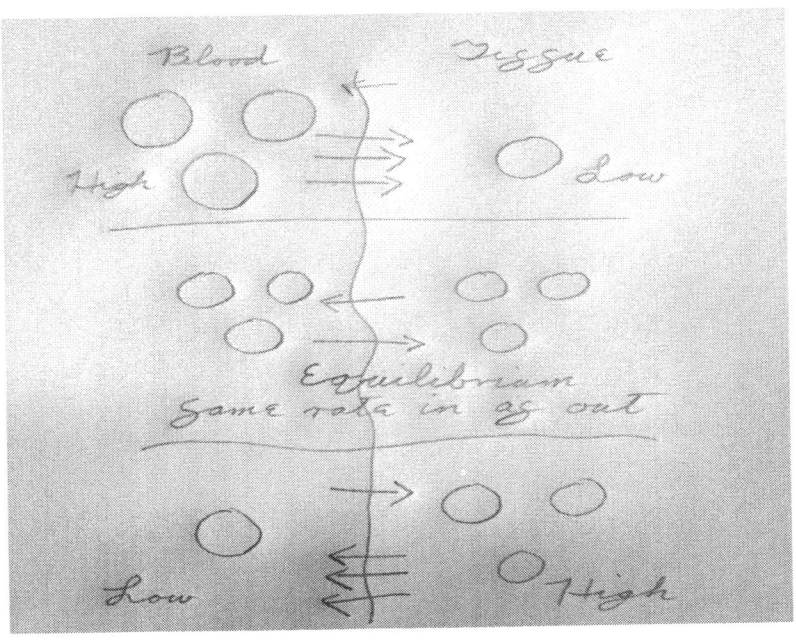

Chapter 9

Oxygen window

Gas will dissolve in and out of a tissue due to the pressure difference (supersaturation or ratio difference) of the gas in the blood and the tissue.

Since the pressure of the gas in the blood is related to the inspired pressure, if we reduce the inspired pressure (ascent or change inspired gas) the gas in the tissue will start to dissolve out of the tissue when the pressure in the tissue is higher than that of the same gas in the blood.

This is the basics behind decompression. However, we can speed up the off-gassing by creating a larger pressure difference by lowering the fraction of inert gas breathed and possibly raising the oxygen percentage (called the oxygen window, inherent unsaturation or partial pressure vacancy).

Oxygen window is what drives inert gas elimination and increases linearly as partial pressures of oxygen increases up to around 2.12 ata where it levels off, however the level is determined by blood flow to any tissue and tissue metabolism.

Oxygen window history

Retired US Captain and physician Albert Richard Behnke (August 8, 1903 to January 16, 1992) was the first person to use the term 'oxygen window' (1967).

Behnke distinguished the symptoms between arterial gas embolism (AGE) from those of decompression sickness (DCS) and suggested the use of oxygen for the treatment of both AGE and DCS (recompression therapy).

How oxygen window works

Partial pressure values in tissue are normally expressed in millimeters of mercury (mmHg), and 1 ata equals around 760 mmHg.

Although dry air has a PO_2 of 159 mmHg at 1 ata it drops to 103 mmHg by the time it reaches the alveoli in the lungs. Due to ventilation and perfusion in the lungs not being perfect, all the blood flowing through the lungs does not undergo gas exchange. Blood that underwent gas exchange and blood that did not do mix later, lowering the arterial PO_2 to around 85 to 95 mmHg.

Note that the O_2 pressure inside a bubble closely follows the surrounding tissue or blood O_2 pressure that the bubble is in.

Unlike other inert gasses CO_2 is transported in the blood not only in a dissolved phase, but also bound to hemoglobin (specialized protein in red blood cells), the same as O_2. Thus for inert gasses the amount of gas present in the blood is directly related to the gas partial pressure. However, O_2 bound to hemoglobin does not contribute to the PO_2 as it is no longer in the dissolved phase, thus dropping the PO_2 in the blood.

During metabolism some of the O_2 in the tissues is converted to CO_2, lowering arterial O_2 partial pressures in the blood as O_2 from the blood enters the tissue to replace the lost O_2. Although roughly the same volume of CO_2 is produced as O_2 used, the CO_2 entering the blood from the tissues will have a lower partial pressure due to its higher solubility than O_2 (around 25 times depending on the tissue). The drop in pressure difference is called the 'Oxygen window'. Oxygen gradient is then large and inwards while CO_2 gradient will be outwards, however small.

At 1 ata and breathing air, the PO_2 difference is around 50 mmHg between arterial and venous blood. The PCO_2 increase from arterial to venous blood however is only around 5 mmHg.

Anton Swanepoel

Thus 'Oxygen window' is when the O2 removed from arterial blood is only partially replaced by CO2 in venous blood and the size of the window is dependent on the arterial PO2 and tissue oxygen consumption.

Since the hemoglobin can bind a large amount of O2, there is only a small amount of O2 dissolved in the blood (a PO2 of around 3 ata is needed to saturate hemoglobin). The dissolved O2 in the blood is used to replace metabolized O2 in tissue and is in turn itself replaced by O2 released from hemoglobin creating a reasonable stable O2 pressure in the arterial blood, one reason why enriched air breathing is seen to be not so much the increased O2 breathed but the reduced inspired nitrogen.

Raising the fraction of oxygen

So what happens if you were to breathe 100% O2 at 1 ata? When breathing O2 at 1 ata (optimal conditions), the PO2 in arterial blood would be around 500 mmHg. When the blood now moves through tissue, the same amount of O2 is extracted, thus the PO2 falls to 57 mmHg in venous blood creating an under saturation of 518 mmHg during O2 breathing at 1 ata. Thus the oxygen window would be 518 mmHg.

Breathing oxygen under elevated pressures

If one were to breathe O2 at 20 fsw then the PO2 inspired would be 1.6 ata (1216 mmHg). The PO2 in the arterial blood would rise to 961 mmHg, yet the same amount of O2 is removed and the venous PO2 would be around 150 mmHg. Thus a large oxygen window is created (1066 mmHg).

Breathing O2 at 10 fsw instead of 20 fsw, the oxygen window is reduced to 844 mmHg (-222 mmHg), creating a smaller partial pressure vacancy in venous blood for non-metabolic gasses to occupy.

Note that inert gas elimination is independent of depth during oxygen breathing but controlled by the gas partial pressure in the tissue and in arterial blood.

Maximum oxygen windows size

When the PO2 in arterial blood exceeds 1600 mmHg, the oxygen window will reach a maximum value of around 1400 mmHg and does not normally increase above this point; additional increase in inspired PO2 will not increase the oxygen window.

When a gas mixture with less than 100% O2 is breathed, inert gas will take up some of the oxygen window size. The amount that the inert gas would occupy depends on the tissue inert partial pressure and inspired partial pressure difference. The larger the difference in negative pressure (tissue pressure being more than inspired pressure) the more gas would diffuse from the tissue into the blood and the oxygen window would be reduced by an amount equal to the pressure of the inert gas in the venous blood.

Oxygen window affects DCS bubbles greatly and is a major factor in the speed of bubble shrinkage, it could prevent the transformation of bubble nuclei into stable bubbles. A bubble can shrink ten times faster when breathing oxygen than air (at sea or hyperbaric pressures, at altitude it can increase to as much as 50 times).

Interestingly, oxygen up to around 2 ata partial pressure is an innocuous (having no adverse effect) replacement for inert gasses, however at higher partial pressures oxygen itself assumes some of the DCS potency of inert gas and can result in O2 DCS from O2 bubbles (does normally resolve fast on its own).

Oxygen window differences in tissue

Oxygen windows differ between tissues due to their oxygen partial pressures, blood flow and metabolic rate of the tissue.

Anton Swanepoel

The kidney cortex has a low oxygen window as it has a high blood flow and high oxygen pressure but a low metabolic rate. The heart and other exercising muscles have a relatively low blood flow compared to their metabolic rate and thus have a low oxygen partial pressure and large oxygen window.

CO2 and oxygen window

In a poorly perfused tissue (possibly due to damage or restriction from a tight computer strap or wetsuit), CO_2 can build up and possibly dilute the bubble inert gas enough to slow inert gas elimination and even cause a shrinking bubble to enlarge.

Counter diffusion and oxygen window

If a second inert gas is inside a bubble, tissue or inspired gas and the exit rate of any inert gas from the bubble is lower than the entrance rate for the inspired inert gas into the bubble, then the bubble will grow in size.

It should be noted that Helium solubility in fatty tissue (such as spinal column) is less than that of nitrogen. Thus if a nitrogen bubble was inside a fatty tissue and the person was given a gas mix containing helium to breathe, then the bubble will normally shrink in size. This is the theory behind neurological DCS treatment where heliox (helium and oxygen) mix is given to a patient to breathe (not normally done for muscle pain only DCS or non air DCS due to the risk of bubbles in tissues other than fat possibly enlarging, however it would be better to suffer from a muscle bend than a spinal bend).

Note, another reason to use a heliox mix is due to oxygen toxicity. If the bubbles are large, then it would take an increased pressure to shrink them to give immediate pain relief and allow blood flow to resume to tissues thus helping to prevent necrosis.

Chapter 10

Bubble talk

In bubble dynamics, there are a number of terms used that can sometimes be confusing or confused with other terms, making understanding of decompression and bubbles difficult.

Following are a few terms with some explanation of them. Note that not all terms are listed here as others are explained elsewhere in the book in more detail, in addition to some of the terms used in bubble dynamics being outside the scope of this book. This section is then just to give the reader a starting understanding of some of the terms used.

Gas nuclei

Gas nuclei are shown to exist in tissue without pressure change and are actually a daily occurrence and natural phenomena. The nuclei are surrounded by a membrane that is permeable thus gas can diffuse in and out, yet the membrane protects the gas bubble from collapse. These nuclei are thought to be able to expand under certain conditions and form larger bubbles that play a role in decompression sickness (DCS). Gas nuclei will be discussed in more detail later.

Venous gas embolism

Venous gas embolism (VGE) is an objective expression (normally in the form of a bubble score) of the existence of decompression stress. This score gives an indication of the amount of bubbles detected in the venous side of the lungs that was transported by the blood from peripherals (legs, arms, etc) of the body to the lungs. There has to date not been an exact link made between VGE scores and DCS, although it is generally thought that a higher VGE score carries a higher DCS risk.

Anton Swanepoel

Dr Valerie Flook in 1998 listed five tissues with a time constant faster than muscle. It was noted from tests that these tissues will always saturate during a 30 minute exposure. These five compartments contribute around 80% of the venous blood when no exercise is done. From the remaining 20% blood, 65% comes from the muscles followed by 25% from fat. Thus it is seen that in short exposures with adequate decompression the muscles are in most cases the source of venous bubbles, and on longer exposures the fat tissue is a major contributor to venous bubbles.

VGE severity index

VGE scores are not always uniform over a time period (score may be high 20 minutes after a dive and drop dramatically later, or be low shortly after a dive and progressively rise with time). An index system was created to improve the usefulness of VGE scores. There are a number of indexes and the way they are calculated is not always the same. One system is the DCIEM severity index that uses a number of VGE scores over a two hour period and averages the scores to come up with a severity index.

Bubble growth index

Bubble growth index (BGI) is a theoretical function that traces the dive profile such as depth, time, gasses used and decompression. It is used in table design and has shown to have a close correlation with DCS incidences.

Absolute inert gas supersaturation

Absolute inert gas supersaturation (also known as Delta P) is the total pressure difference between the calculated inert gas partial pressure in a tissue and the ambient pressure, and is considered a large factor in gas phase expansion. The Delta P is worked out for each tissue M (maximum) value.

Relative inert gas supersaturation

Relative inert gas supersaturation is the pressure difference between the calculated inert gas partial pressure in a tissue (for each M-value) and the maximum tolerable supersaturation values as pre-defined for that tissue M-value. Faster tissue can handle a larger pressure gradient than slower tissue. The maximum value used is then the theoretical pressure gradient that is thought would not result in bubble formation in a tissue.

Potential decompression stress

This relates to the time course of bubble growth and the maximum expected size of bubbles over time after decompression exposure if a rapid reduction in ambient pressure was experienced (sudden surface).

Exposure index

This is an index expressing the pressure times square root of the time of exposure. This creates a single number for each dive depth and bottom time combination and relates to inert gas uptake for a dive pattern and its potential risk for DCS. Note that different depth and time exposures can have the same number and the number should be used with other indexes to create safe decompression profiles.

Arterial gas embolism

Arterial gas embolism (AGE) is when bubbles are found in the arterial side of the lungs. This can be due to a number of reasons, from the lungs being overloaded with bubbles and some made it through, lung shunting, lung rupture, PFO and ASD. These bubbles do travel to the rest of the body (normally the heart, spinal column and brain first) and are thought to play a major role in DCS.

Chapter 11

Pre existing bubbles

Pre existing bubbles, micro bubbles or bubble seeds are thought to play a major role in DCS. The theory is that there are bubbles already in a diver's body before a dive (not necessarily from a previous dive) that can grow during the course of a dive. However, no direct link between nuclei and DCS has been found or proven, and in some cases bubble formation due to other mechanisms seems to play a larger role than nuclei.

Bubble nuclei are small enough to remain in solution, yet are strong enough not to collapse due to an elastic skin composed of surface active molecules. The skin is normally permeable to gas, however with rapid large increases in ambient pressure (around 8 atm) the skin may become impermeable. The skin allows the bubble to exist where normally the bubble would have dissolved within a few seconds. If the pressure is enough then the skin will crumble (crush depth) and the gas in the skin will dissolve into the surrounding tissue.

Nuclei history

E. Newton Harvey (1887-1959) was the first to observe and reason the existence of gas nuclei. Harvey studied decompression illness (DCI) during World War II and noted fluid micronuclei in water around an ultrasound transducer. The energy from the ultrasound was not thought to be enough to cause spontaneous microbubbles thus Harvey reasoned that micronuclei must already exist in the fluid.

How bubbles form

It is thought that there are two principal mechanisms how bubbles can form, by gas nuclei (micro small pre existing bubbles), and by their own (from nothing, also called spontaneous bubbles).

-Spontaneous bubbles

Depending on the inert gas and supersaturation of the inert gas, from 120 to 360 ata is needed to form bubbles from nothing. If microbubbles were not present in a diver it is reasoned that a diver could dive to around 1000 m (3300 ft) or more and come directly to the surface without needing to decompress. That would be cool.

-Nuclei bubbles

Bubbles forming from gas nuclei need only tenths of atmospheres (as low as 0.5 to 0.7 ata difference), and it is thought that inert gas supersaturation is the driving force for bubble formation and growth.

-Bubble formation and depth

The critical supersaturation trigger point when bubbles form is ambient pressure independent, a reduction from 300ft or 30ft where the critical supersaturation pressure is exceeded, can trigger bubble formation. However, once the threshold has been exceeded and bubbles formed, the amount and size of the bubbles seem to be exposure pressure dependent.

Where do gas nuclei come from?

Bubbles are normally first seen in peripheral veins, and the theory is that these venous bubbles if in significant quantity can lead to arterial bubbles.

-Fluid fracturing

Nuclei are thought to form from viscous adhesion that generates negative pressures (being hundreds of atmospheres in magnitude) during relative motion of tissue structures. It is thought to require a negative pressure of around 1,400 ata to form nuclei.

Anton Swanepoel

The motion causes a bubble formation that is mechanical in nature (not due to gas uptake) and is called tribonucleation (also called vacuum phenomena (VP) and first noted in 1910 by Frick).

Basically the fluid is ripped apart (fracturing) and tiny holes or bubbles form. Think of stretching a rubber band, at a point it will break. The same effect happens with fluid when it is subjected to a vacuum. The parts of the joints move away from each other and the lubricating fluid inbetween the joints is subjected to a vacuum that can cause the fluid to split apart.

The strength of the fluid to resist vacuum bubbles from forming is called the tensile strength of the fluid. This fracturing of liquid is also the limiting factor on how high a vacuum pump can suck water up a pipe, and is the reason to rather use a pressure pump to push water up.

The vacuum bubble does have some molecules of the liquid it is in, inside the bubble. If additional molecules from gas diffuse into the bubble the pressure increases, if the internal pressure inside the bubble equals the outside pressure then the bubble is stable. A cool trick to make microbubbles grow spontaneously is to drop some uncoated Mentos sweets into diet Coca Cola. WARNING, do not do this to your partner's drink at a dinner table unless you are looking for trouble.

-Homogeneous and heterogeneous nucleation
There are two forms of vapor bubbles, being homogeneous nucleation and heterogeneous nucleation. Homogeneous nucleation is when vapor bubbles are created away from bounding walls and in the absence of any foreign material. Heterogeneous nucleation is when vapor bubbles are formed on cavities or scratches on a surface bounding a liquid.

-Tribonucleation

Tribonucleation (named by Hayward) creates gas cavities that can be detected by x-ray and GT-scans and is seen in almost every joint and also in the spine. The same force can cause a water vapor bubble to form.

This bubble would normally disappear as soon as the force was removed, unless a gas diffuses into it before it disappears (both O_2 and CO_2 are always readily available and for the most part, so is N_2 and possibly He).

Tribonucleation can create vaporous or gaseous cavitation. Gas cavitation creates a gas filled bubble that lasts longer than a vapor bubble, although it is possible for inert gas to dissolve into the vapor (vacuum) bubble, forming a gas filled bubble.

Common bubble in diving

Non spontaneous bubble formation (normally from gaseous nuclei) is the most common problem in diving. These nuclei can have either a 'shell' or 'skin' that protects the bubble from being crushed. The bubble can be gas trapped in cracks, crevices and scratches in the walls (such as arterial tissue walls in contact with blood), or be gas in suspended particles. Interestingly, the gas bubbles in soft drinks (fizzy drinks) originate from these nuclei.

The skin that protects the gas in the nuclei may form from macromolecules present in the solution and has the characteristics of being flexible enough to allow the nuclei to expand or contract as the gas dissolves into and out of the nuclei while being strong enough to resist crushing.

Anton Swanepoel

-Crevice nuclei

Crevice nuclei are thought to originate the fastest from conical formed crevices with either straight or elliptical curved walls. Crevices that are negatively concaved shaped at the liquid interface normally always enlarge bubbles and can continually form bubbles.

Knuckle cracking

Knuckle cracking causes vaporous capitation (bubble formation) where vapor filled bubbles are created in a vacuum and collapse with noise as the negative pressure is removed. Note that not all the bubbles may disappear so knuckle cracking on decompression or diving for that matter can possibly increase DCS risk. When nitrogen is removed from the tissues due to oxygen breathing, joint cracking becomes more pronounced and painful.

Vacuum phenomena increase with age in the spine and suggest some reason for the increase in DCS risk with age, in addition to raising the question if a spinal injury increases DCS risk.

An eye for bubbles

Recent examination and study on microvessel damage of diver's retinas has shown that the eye may be a primary site of bubble formation on ascent. The eye being an extension of the brain has also been found to be affected by lesions the same as the brain.

Gas phase formers

Gas phase former tissue is tissue that is seen to have the ability to form bubbles, these are normally tissues that can be active such as muscle, tendons, ligaments, fat tissue and possibly the spinal column. It is thought that since the tissue can move, nuclei can form in the tissue and thus lead to bubble formation.

Gas phase receivers

Gas phase receiver tissue is tissue that is seen not to produce bubbles, but is at the receiving end of bubbles created elsewhere. Tissues include the lungs, brain, fetal organs, the heart, venous blood and possibly the spinal column. The lungs are normally the terminal point for bubbles while the venous blood normally receives most of the bubbles from peripherals.

The fetus has no filters as the lungs are not yet working, thus any bubbles that reach the fetus can affect the fetus brain and spinal column (could be venous bubbles that do not affect the mother). This is one of the main reasons not to dive while being pregnant.

Tissue bubbles

It is recognized that a bubble may form in a tissue close to a blood vessel and that due to pressure difference in inert gas on ascent, gas in the tissue may migrate to the blood vessel and form a bubble on the blood vessel wall (around a nuclei site) and cause mechanical disruption of the blood vessel.

If the bubble grows large enough it can get detached from the blood vessel wall and be transported to the lungs (hopefully to be filtered out before it affects the body). If the bubble stays in the tissue, then it may grow for some time depending on the tissue saturation and can cause damage to the surrounding tissue. If the bubble is close to small blood vessels it could possibly compress them and stop blood flow. If the time of compression is long enough then ischemic damage may be done to the tissue (tissue death). Since the bubble is not moving, it will not show up on Doppler monitoring.

Anton Swanepoel

Compression of nuclei

In tests done by McDonough and Hemmingsen it was found that bubbles formed in marine animals at 2 ata supersaturation when the animal moved, there were no bubbles detected even at 50 ata supersaturation when the animal was immobile.

Gas nuclei can be reduced by pressure increase such as diving, called adaption. Nuclei are thought to take up to a week to regenerate (reason for the seven days adaption period in tests).

This is one of the reasons why it is thought that dive instructors doing frequent dives are less prone to DCS than occasional divers. It is thought that with frequent diving as with dive masters and instructors diving every day that DCS risk drops by about 50% in the first month after starting active work and drops again by around 50% after another three months of active diving.

Exercise and nuclei

Exercise (especially when applying pressure to the joints such as weight lifting) before and during a dive will promote nuclei creation and increase the risk of bubble formation and DCS. If nuclei are formed at depth then the nuclei will be formed with the surrounding tissue gas pressure, thus the risk of bubble formation and DCS is greatly increased.

Pressure needed to crush nuclei

Not all nuclei are crushed on descent though, it is thought that a pressure of around 10 ata (300 ft) is needed to crush most nuclei, however in ICD tests done it was found that some nuclei remained stable even at 38 ata (1200 fsw).

Tests on shrimp showed a reduction in nuclei after a brief pressure treatment before altitude decompression. Evans and Walder pressurized shrimp to 389 ata before altitude decompression and saw a marked reduction in nuclei. Daniels pre-pressurized shrimp to 200 ata before altitude decompression at 53 000 ft and noted bubble formation drop from 3.5 to 0.5 bubbles per shrimp compared to no pre-pressurization.

In other tests with rats where they were exposed (briefly) to a hydrostatic pressure equivalent to 600 ft before being exposed to a 240 ft dive showed a 74% fatal rate, compared to 83% without the treatment.

Bubble dissolve rate

Note that although it is generally thought that one is desaturated in around 48 hours, it takes around four to eight hours to get rid of most of the bubbles and that some may persist for longer if they are large. Thus make your second dive conservative.

Haldane recognized this and suggested that tunnel workers be exposed to gradual increase in pressure and exposure time. In observations on tunnel workers by Walder it was noted that DCS incidence fell from 12 to 3% after a 10 day period involving a daily exposure, and to between 1 and 2% after that. However, the results were specific for each exposure, and on deeper exposures the risk returned to normal.

In tests done on divers breathing heliox with 0.7 ata PPO2 at 120 ft for 20 minutes a marked reduction in bubble scores were noted on subsequent dives. The divers did three dives and each dive was separated by five days of rest.

Anton Swanepoel

Boiling water and bubbles

Water boils at around 100ºC at sea level due to gas nuclei, in their absence water can be heated to around 280 ºC at sea level without bubbles forming.

The more pressure the water is under, the hotter it can be before bubbles form and is the reason why motorcars can run at a hotter temperature than 100 ºC without the water in the radiator boiling as it is under pressure; also the reason water boils at a lower temperature at altitude as it is under less pressure than at sea level.

Fish bubble disease

Extensive studies have been done on fish dying from nitrogen bubbles in their gills in dams. It was found that the fish swimming below dams were subjected to entrained nitrogen at a slight supersaturation due to the falling of water. With the constant movement of swimming, bubbles would form in their gills after several hours that eventually proved fatal to the fish. The result was to redesign dams so that the falling water does not entrain as much nitrogen.

Bubble re-growth after compression from descent

As a diver descends, the gas nuclei are compressed until the bubble seed crushes or the descent is halted. If the bubble did not crush, then gas will diffuse into the bubble from the surrounding tissue according to the gas gradient (pressure between the gas in the bubble and that of the tissue).

-Short bottom times

On short bottom times the bubble will not grow much and will expand to the original size (or close to it) on ascent.

It is theorized that in these cases, adding a deep stop will only allow possible additional on-gassing and possibly increased bubble size. This could explain why some dives with deep stops had higher VGE scores than dives without deep stops.

-Longer bottom times

For longer bottom times, the bubble will re-grow at the bottom according to the time spent at the bottom. At total saturation the bubble may be the same size as it was on the surface, however with increased density. On ascent, the bubble will expand as ambient pressure is lessened. Gas will diffuse out of the bubble into local tissue and blood if the pressure in the bubble is greater and the speed is slow enough, else the bubble may grow in size.

Bubble expansion on ascent

If the bubble size grew sufficiently at the bottom part of the dive, and the gas in the bubble is not given enough time to diffuse out of the bubble, then the bubble can expand on ascent to a size that may play a role in DCS. In these cases it is then theorized that adding deep stops or slowing the ascent speed may give the gas enough time to diffuse out of the bubble so that the bubble either remains at a risk free size or possibly shrink in size.

Bubble linking

It is possible for bubbles to link up and form a larger bubble. The new bubble if large enough may get stuck in the tissues or blood vessels and restrict blood flow. The bubble can only shrink once the local tissue gas pressure is lower than the bubble pressure. However, as a bubble grows, the surface tension is reduced and so too the internal pressure. Thus even if two bubbles had the same pressure as the surrounding tissue, if linked up the new bubble may have an internal pressure lower than the surrounding tissue, gas will then dissolve into the bubble, increasing its size.

Anton Swanepoel

Microbubbles and RGBM

Microbubbles also form the basis for the RGBM recommendation to do the deep dive first. Since recreational deep dives are short dives, the dive will crush many of the micro bubbles and extinguish many nucleation sites. The bubbles will also not have time to re-grow at depth and those that were not crushed will expand on ascent to almost original size.

On subsequent dives, the dives need to be shallower than the crush depth of the first dive to allow the risk for excitation of smaller micronuclei to be reduced.

Longer bottom time on subsequent dives may allow bubble seeds to grow at depth, however since there are now fewer of these bubbles and since the number of micronuclei that can lead to bubbles are reduced, the risk for bubbles forming that can lead to DCS is reduced.

Microbubbles and VPM

From tests done on sea, tap and distilled water it was noted that cavitation (bubbles forming) needs more than modest changes in pressure and the random motion of water and gas molecules to occur.

Further tests have demonstrated that the thresholds for cavitation can be raised by degassing or by application of static pressure. It is thus concluded that the precocious onset of cavitation in aqueous media generally is due to the presence of bubble nuclei. It was thought that gas bubbles larger than 1 micron would float to the surface of a standing liquid and any smaller bubbles would dissolve back into the liquid within a few seconds (due to surface tension), however in tests this was shown not to be the case.

A new decompression model was needed as normal tissue loading models do not track micro bubbles, thus the Varying-permeability model (VPM) was introduced.

Bubbles and Doppler

A theory was put forward that the Doppler device itself can cause bubble formation. This is based on bubbles forming due to vibrations that have been shown to create bubbles (normally the vibrations found in helicopters).

The Doppler device normally used by the French has an electric power of 140 milliwatt, this results in an acoustic power of 40 milliwatt. However, due to tissue absorption, only around 4 milliwatt reaches the heart.

Tests were done using 4 watts of ultrasound energy at the same frequency as the Doppler device, relating to a 1000 times stronger output. No bubbles were detected and it was concluded that the Doppler devices do not cause bubbles to form.

Correlation between bubble scores and DCS

Although venous gas embolism (VGE) bubble scores have been and are used in many studies to test for the effectiveness of new dive profiles, there has been no direct link found between bubble scores and DCS incidences.

What has been noted however is that DCS risk does rise with a higher bubble score, although the score cannot predict the incidence of DCS.

Anton Swanepoel

It was found that DCS risk is around 1% with a KM bubble score between one and two, and that DCS risk is around 13% for bubble scores of four. In light of this, NASA has adopted an approve/reject basis using VGE bubble scores. The cutoff reject point is where any table or profile produces 20% or more VGE four scores.

Depth changes and bubble formation

Depth changes during bottom time are one of the factors which can contribute to the extent of decompression bubble formation. In 1997, Jacobsen did a report on 2622 saturation dives and found a relationship between the incidence of DCI and the number of depth changes during the saturation period.

Assuming bubbles from nuclei are already in the system in addition to some being created at depth, then if the diver descends deeper than the normal bottom depth those bubbles may increase in size when the diver ascends back up to the original bottom depth.
The time at the increased depth and the speed of ascent back to the original bottom depth is thus very important.

A faster ascent rate causes the highest volume of gas in bubbles, especially in the brain. Slowing the return down can reduce the brain gas to 75% or less. Note that increased levels of oxygen from increased partial pressures on descent may cause local transient reductions in blood flow during which that portion of the brain will not be able to offload gas and bubbles may form, once formed they will not resolve when blood flow returns to normal. A slower return gives the brain extra protection.

-Repeated depth changes

Any bubbles remaining from a previous depth change will be recompressed on descending to a deeper depth, and any gas leaving the bubble would diffuse into local tissues.

Additional gas will be taken up at the increased depth that may not be calculated for by dive tables. Although computers will calculate the additional gas uptake, if the ascent back to the original bottom depth was fast enough to allow bubbles to form, the decompression calculation can be out (bubbles in the system slows off-gassing).

If the depth change is upwards, then due to the lessened ambient pressure, bubbles can potentially form or grow if the pressure change is large and fast enough. This could be from a possible stuck inflator valve, loss of weights or other gear such as loss of a decompression tank.

DCS risk increases considerably when the drop to a deeper depth and return to the original depth is followed by termination of the bottom part of the dive and final ascent is started. Thus bouncing down and up at the end of the bottom part just to record a deeper bottom depth for ego's sake is a very bad idea.

If a bounce down had to be done, then the DCS risk can be reduced by increasing the time at the bottom before ascending, possibly going to overrun tables or by slowing the return, as starting decompression while bubbles are present adds a significant risk for DCS.

Chapter 12

ICD and bubbles

Deep tissue counter diffusion occurs when any different inert gasses are breathed in sequence, such as switching to different travel mixes or deco mixes. There are two possibilities here, supersaturation or subsaturation.

-Supersaturation

In supersaturation a diver switches from a slower equilibrating inert gas to a higher equilibrating inert gas. The higher equilibrating gas enters the tissues faster than the replaced inert gas leaves the tissue. The total pressure in the tissues will rise (this happens independent of depth changes). Any bubbles that are present have a higher chance of growing.

Subsaturation

Subsaturation is when a switch from a higher equilibrating inert gas to a lower equilibrating inert gas is made. The new inert gas enters the tissue slower than the replaced inert gas leaves the tissue and thus the gradient for the faster inert gas is greater, speeding up the release of the inert gas. This can speed up decompression and is used in some technical, military, scientific and commercial diving. However the risk exists that should too large a gradient be created, bubbles may form, especially from fast inert gasses such as helium.

Both situations can be favorable in the right conditions, however the right calculations need to be done for safe switching. For more calculations on ICD, see 'Dive Computers' and 'The Art of Gas Blending' by Anton Swanepoel

www.antonswanepoelbooks.com/dive_computers.php
www.antonswanepoelbooks.com/the_art_of_gas_blending.php

During hyperbaric treatment a 50/50 heliox mix is sometimes used to treat DCS caused by air diving. The reason is that the diver can be pressurized deeper than with pure oxygen to relieve symptoms, and no additional nitrogen will be taken up, as the case would be had the diver been recompressed on air.

Although helium will diffuse into the tissues, it is less soluble thus less volume of gas will defuse in, and it is also a faster diffusion gas than nitrogen. The risk of bubbles forming is less on helium than nitrogen for the rate of ascent used in recompression therapy. A 50/50 recompression has actually been shown to be the most effective treatment by the Israeli Naval Hyperbaric Institute for treating air DCS cases.

In decompression for deep air dives, a switch to a heliox mix in tests on pigs at Trondheim showed that the bubble score just after the dive was the same as had no switch been made, however the bubbles cleared in most cases after only 1½ hours for the helium switch, where they were still detectable up to 16 hours after surfacing for the air only decompression.

In other tests heliox switches have been shown to reduce or eliminate bubbles after decompression from a deep air dive (the switch is normally done at around 20 to 30 m, 99 ft). The best result however was found to use a light tri-mix 30/20/50 followed by oxygen decompression for the deep air dive profiles tested.

Chapter 13

Factors that can affect decompression

There are a number of factors that may affect off-gassing; following are a number of those influences.

Thermal change and decompression

It is well known that divers routinely get cold on dives (especially when wearing wetsuits), some may not actually feel cold, but the body temperature may have dropped. What then is the effect of thermal changes on diving?

Studies done by the US Navy on thermal changes had Navy working decompression dives compared to Caribbean recreational divers and Scapa Flow wreck divers to note the effect of thermal changes on decompression and DCS risk.

-Cold to warm

When Navy divers were cold on the bottom part of the dive and warm on the decompression part of the dive they had the same risk of DCS as Caribbean recreational divers even though they were doing decompression diving and worked at depth.

-Warm to warm

On dives where the diver remained at the same temperature during both the bottom part and decompression part of the dive, the risk increased by 15 times compared to 'cold to warm' divers. It should be noted that one of the possibilities for the higher DCS risk on 'warm to warm' dives could be dehydration and heat stress.

-Cold to cold

Navy divers that were cold on both the bottom part and the decompression part of the dive had a 20 times increased DCS risk than 'cold to warm' divers.

-Warm to cold

The most stressful conditions and highest risk of DCS was when the diver was warm on the bottom working part of the dive and cold on the decompression part of the dive.

When the body is immersed in cold water or becomes cold in the dive, vasoconstriction occurs and blood is pooled away from the extremities to the internal organs to try and conserve heat. This may affect local tissue washout of inert gas. Even though whole body inert gas washout may seem to be unaffected, a local tissue may contain enough diffused inert gas to cause DCS on surfacing.

From tests it was noted that in some cases nitrogen in local tissues that was washed out after two hours on air decompression, were only 1/3 washed out when decompression was done in cold water.

-Conclusion for thermal change

From the tests done, it is clear that being warm on the bottom and cold on the decompression is not ideal for decompression. It is suggested not to do work on the bottom that will exert you, and not to stay still and get cold on decompression. By doing slight exercise (light finning) may help circulation and help keep your muscles warm.

Having a proper exposure suit to help you not lose too much heat is a must. In commercial and military diving, warm water suits are sometimes used if decompression is done in the water. Some divers modify motorcycle electric underwear, pants and jackets for diving (using a drysuit). The gear utilizes a small 12volt battery that can be housed in a sealed container. The electricity is left off on the bottom part of the dive and then switched on, on the decompression part of the dive.

Note, CCR divers recycle the breathing gas and lose less heat normally than OC divers. The scrubber material that interacts with the CO_2 in the loop creates additional heat that in turn will help keep the diver warmer.

As the scrubber, loop gas and unit itself heats up over time from the diver breathing and the chemical reaction in the scrubber unit, it will affect decompression differently than an OC diver doing the same dive, possibly creating a more favorable DCS risk for the CCR diver compared to the OC diver who may be getting colder.

Head down tilt position

Cardiac output increases with a head down tilt position, this in turn may increase perfusion to tissues as blood flow is increased, especially in fatty tissue as fatty tissue blood flow is linked to arterial blood pressure. A fast descent to the bottom with a head down position stresses the heart immensely.

Exercise

With exercise, cardiac output is raised that increases blood flow to tissues, especially to the muscles to keep up with oxygen demand and helps to keep the muscles warm.

-Exercise at deco stops

Although increased blood flow to the muscles may increase inert gas elimination at decompression, too much exercise may result in blood being shifted to the muscles and away from other tissues.

Blood flow may then be restricted to fatty tissue that can contain more inert gas and hamper inert gas elimination, increasing DCS risk. With heavy exercise nuclei creation is also increased.

Note that light exercise at decompression is only favorable if no bubbles are present, as exercise greatly increases the risk of DCS when bubbles are present. In saturation diving there is always bubbles present thus the reverse is true for saturation diving, exercise at decompression stops increases DCS risk.

This is normally why deep knee bends are done in bubble detection tests. The thought is that bubbles that are stuck on the venous or artery walls may become dislodged with movement, where they go depends on where they come from. Venous bubbles normally go to the lungs, but artery bubbles have already bypassed the lungs and are on their way to the spine, brain and the rest of the body.

Due to nuclei being present at surface levels, astronauts and aviators that will be exposed to altitudes over 10 000 to 18 000 ft need to eliminate nitrogen from the system before altitude exposure, normally by pre-breathing oxygen (same concept as decompression stops, eliminating inert gas).

For the Apollo program the shuttle was at 14.7 psi with air as a breathing mix, while the extravehicular activity (EVA) suits were 4.3 psi with oxygen as a breathing mix. When astronauts pre-breathed oxygen for four hours before EVA activity a 20% mild DCS incidence was reported, however with eight hours of pre-breathing at rest or 3.5 hours of pre-breathing while doing exercise, DCS problems were eliminated.

From tests it seems that light to mild continuous exercise at decompression does not increase bubble formation, where heavy or intermittent exercise does.

-Exercise at depth
Exercising at depth and after decompression greatly increases DCS risk.

In a study by Bühlmann and Schibli in 1972 it was found that divers that did work at depth needed around 20 to 44% more decompression than resting divers.

A study done by the Medical Operations Branch, NASA-Johnson Space Center, Houston found that decompression-induced bubble formation significantly increases if lower extremity exercise is performed just prior to depressurization. The longer the rest period before pressure is reduced, the less bubbles formed.

Tests done on divers to 60 ft for 60 minutes where they either rested or did exercise at the bottom showed an increase of 20% nitrogen load for the divers that exercised. However, when divers were taken to 100 ft for 25 minutes and either exercised or not, an increase of 60% was seen in nitrogen load for the divers that exercised. (Nitrogen load is the amount of nitrogen they off-gas after the dive.)

-Exercise after decompression

Exercise after decompression is highly discouraged as this can lead to an increased risk of DCS. Van Der Aue found an increase of 34% in DCS in divers who lifted 25 lbs weights for 2 hours after no decompression dives compared to non exercise groups (weight of a standard 80 cubic feet scuba tank is around 35 lbs). Depths tested were 40, 100 and 150 ft.

In a study done in the 1940s it was found that DCS incidence rose by around 32% in subjects doing 5 push ups and 5 knee bends every 15 minutes after decompressing to 38 000 ft.

-Fitness exercise

Exercise such as swimming causes a total body increase in blood flow, where weight lifting causes an interruption in blood flow that is followed by a sudden compensatory surge in blood flow when the muscles are relaxed again, and when this sudden blood flow may dislodge bubbles on venous or arterial walls. The constant movement (light) keeps blood flow up that helps inert gas diffusion.

Fitness and DCS

In studies for fitness and DCS, students who participated in vigorous sports such as basketball, weight training, stair climbing and long-distance running were compared. All the mentioned exercises except long-distance running were seen to increase the risk of DCS (especially if done before or after a dive) as they may increase nuclei formation and predispose to bubble formation. Subjects that did heavy exercises such as weight lifting had a significantly greater DCS incidence than the subjects that did aerobic exercise such as long-distance running.

Aerobic exercise such as long-distance running or swimming is seen to raise the basal metabolic rate and may increase nitrogen elimination on decompression and reduce DCS risk. It should not be seen that doing anaerobic exercise places one at increased risk, but that having a higher basal metabolic rate reduces DCS risk.

Hypoxia

Mild hypoxia stimulates blood circulation and ventilation and could increase inert gas elimination. Although it is reported that artificially induced mild hypoxia reduces the symptoms of altitude DCS it is not a safe decompression option, just interesting to note. Thus as you are running out of gas on your deco stop, at least you know you will off-gas a little quicker. ☺

Vasodilation and vasoconstriction

When the body is cold, it constricts the blood flow to the peripherals and pools the blood to the central body cavity in order to save heat. The body can, if it experiences a cold shock, constrict blood flow to half its max constriction almost immediately, hence the reason you can get a heart attack by jumping into cold water.

An old belief is to immerse your arms in cold water first before you jump in to allow the body to sense some cold and not be shocked, this may have some merit. Warmth on the other hand causes vasodilation and increased blood flow.

Hormones causing vasodilation and vasoconstriction

Systemic hormones such as angiotensin (a decapeptide hormone that is formed from the plasma glycoprotein angiotensinogen) and vasopressin (a hormone secreted by cells of the hypothalamic nuclei and stored in the posterior pituitary) cause vasoconstriction.

Kinins, a group of vasoactive straight-chain polypeptides that is formed by kallikrein-catalyzed cleavage of kininogens causes vasodilation in addition to altering vascular permeability. Histamine, amine, $C_5H_9N_3$ that is produced by decarboxylation of histidine and serotonin (5-hydroxytryptamine (5-HT) a hormone and neurotransmitter) cause vasodilation. Note that when you get seasick, the body produces increased amounts of histamine.

Negative pressure breathing

Negative pressure breathing (NPB) has been shown to increase adipose tissue (fat) blood flow and cardiac output (Balldin, 1976).

A 20 cm water negative value increased subcutaneous fat inert gas elimination by around 70%. If oxygen was breathed with NPB (compared to oxygen breathing only) delayed intracardial gas bubbles and reduced DCS risk was noted.

Positive pressure breathing

A positive breathing of 20 cm H20 decreased subcutaneous adipose tissue inert gas elimination by around 40% and lowered cardiac output. This can have a marked reduction in decompression effectiveness.

Use of vasodilators

Although this would not be used by the average diver, certain drugs can cause vasodilation and enhance inert gas off-gassing, possibly in the treatment of DCS in a chamber. Orally administered terbutaline (a sympathomimetic beta 2 receptor) has been shown to increase subcutaneous adipose tissue inert gas elimination by more than 100% (Balldin, 1976).

Increased partial pressure of Oxygen

Due to the pressure gradient of inert gas playing a major role in off-gassing, if one were to raise the gradient by lowering the inspired (breathed) inert gas partial pressure, it will enhance off-gassing (within the limits of oxygen toxicity). Patients in recompression chambers may breathe PPO2 as high as 2 ata and divers decompressing sometimes go as high as 1.6 ata.

Hyperoxia was shown to be able to cause reduced blood flow to muscles in addition to reduced cardiac output (Balldin, Ludgren, Lundvall and Mellander, 1971). In the tests done it was found that CO2 build-up in dead air-spaces may increase the severity of DCS if it has already formed.

Anton Swanepoel

Carotid baroreceptors

Carotid baroreceptors are located in the neck along the sides under the jaw. Blood pressure is detected and partly regulated by these receptors. By wearing a tight wetsuit or drysuit it is possible for the receptors to signal a drop in blood pressure. The drop in blood flow does not just affect blood flow to tissue but potentially cause unconsciousness as the blood pressure and flow can drop too low to supply enough oxygen to the brain.

Immersion

When the body is immersed in cold water, blood is shifted to the core of the body and the central blood volume increases by about 700 ml. This blood is taken from the extremities of the body. The heart has to work harder as cardiac output increases by 30% while systemic vascular resistance (SVR) decreases by 30% (SVR refers to the resistance to blood flow offered by all of the systemic vasculature, excluding the pulmonary vasculature (lungs)).

Tissue perfusion increases with no rise in oxygen consumption, and plasma volume increases as fluids move from the tissues to the vascular space (normally within the first 30 minutes), this leads to diuresis (increased excretion of urine), natriuresis (the process of excretion of sodium in the urine), and kaliuresis (the process of excreting potassium in the urine) after about ½ hour to two hours of immersion. (Arborelius, Balldin, Lilja and Ludgren, 1972)

It has already been noted that decompression differs between subjects in a dry chamber and those decompressing in a wet chamber (cardiac output increases in immersion). However, when subjects were decompression immersed with a head out sitting position, inert gas elimination was 40% higher in the first ½ hour and 30% higher over a two hour period than those that decompressed in a dry chamber. (Balldin and Ludgren, 1972)

It was also noted that surface decompression had a higher DCS risk than in-water decompression. Interestingly, surface decompression on oxygen seemed even more dangerous than air in water decompression, although oxygen decompression is better than air decompression if done in the same environment.

Supine position

When the body is in a supine position, blood circulation to the leg muscles has been noted to rise by 100% and 35% in subcutaneous fat, the overall inert gas elimination in a supine position during oxygen breathing was 24% higher for the first ½ hour and 15% after two hours compared to an erect body position. (Balldin, 1973, 1976)

Thermal changes

Being cold may decrease blood flow and perfusion, however being warm increases blood flow just as markedly. In tests done (Balldin and Ludgren, 1972 and Balldin , 1978) it was shown that raising the temperature two degrees Celsius from 35 to 37 °C raised the mean subcutaneous adipose tissue blood flow by 90% and the total-body inert gas elimination by 6% in two hours.

When the temperature was lowered to 32 °C, a 10% reduction in inert gas elimination was noted. Interestingly, in dry conditions temperature change did not have as big an effect, this could possibly be due to one losing more heat in water than air of the same temperature.

To test thermal changes even more, subjects were placed either in a dry chamber at thermalneutral temperature or immersed in 37 °C water where they breathed oxygen for 25 minutes (denitogenation). The subjects were then taken to a pressure of 155 mmHG or 20.7 Kpa to provoke DCS. Dry chamber subjects had a 90% DCS hit rate compared to immersed subjects having a 20% DCS hit rate. (Balldin, 1973)

Anton Swanepoel

Chapter 14

Bubbles and decompression

Bubbles can actually be seen as a tissue with a high inert gas solubility and gas from the surrounding tissue diffuses into the bubble. When bubbles form, diffusion and perfusion are in series. It is thought that circulating bubbles cause neurological symptoms and stationary bubbles cause articular pain.

If the tissue inert gas pressure is higher than the bubble inert gas pressure then gas will diffuse into the bubble from the surrounding tissue. The pressure in the tissue first needs to drop to below the inert gas pressure in the bubble before gas can diffuse out of the bubble, slowing down decompression. Small bubbles will dissolve faster than bigger bubbles due to surface tension, the surface tension is higher in smaller bubbles, causing the internal gas pressure to rise, thus allowing faster gas transfer.

Oxygen and CO_2 levels in both blood and tissue are kept reasonably stable. When a pressure change occurs, both oxygen and CO_2 levels inside bubbles equilibrate rapidly with its surrounding tissue. Thus both oxygen and CO_2 can in some cases cause bubbles to grow.

Bubble shrink and expand rate

Gas permeability (its diffusion and solubility) affects the rate gas enters or leaves a bubble. If the gas entering the bubble has a higher permeability than the one exiting, then the bubble will grow, called counter diffusion. Nitrous oxide has a higher permeability than nitrogen or helium and causes bubbles to grow rapidly. Although CO_2 has a high permeability it has a low tissue tension. Helium has a higher permeability than nitrogen and a nitrogen bubble will grow if Helium diffuses in.

It should be noted that counter diffusion in lipid (fat) cells such as brain and spinal column is not fully known.

Interestingly, bubble reduction speed in size is not affected by ambient pressure. Thus a bubble will shrink at the same rate after compression as it would before compression.

An equation is used to calculate how long a bubble will take to dissolve when breathing air at the surface. This equation is then modified to try to predict at what rate a bubble will dissolve in the human body. The equation is known as the Epstein-Plesset equation and calculates that dissolution times for an air bubble in water is 1 second for a 1 μm (micron) bubble, 1 to 6 seconds for a 10 μm bubble, 100 to 600 seconds for 100 μm bubble and 1 to 6 million seconds (11 to 70 days) for a 1 mm bubble.

As noted, this equation calculates bubble diffusion in water with a spherical bubble, and in the human body many factors can affect bubble shrinking such as if the bubble changes shape. A cylindrical bubble can take 50% longer to dissolve, not to mention the possibility of additional gasses dissolving into the bubble and pressure changes allowing the bubble to expand. A trapped bubble may not be able to dissolve back into tissue depending on its location.

Bubble size and ambient pressure changes

The volume that molecules from a gas bubble occupy is inversely proportional to ambient pressure, thus at 5 ata, the volume would be 1/5 of the volume of 1 ata. However, the radius or diameter of a bubble does not follow this rule. The radius of a bubble is inversely proportional to the cube root of the ambient pressure. Thus a bubble at 10 ata is around ½ its 1 ata radius. Bubble size in recompression only shrinks marginally compared to the increase in pressure.

The effect of this can be seen in recompression DCS treatment. If a bubble that would take 20 minutes to be eliminated on oxygen breathing is compressed to 3 ata, then the bubble will only shrink 30%. Since the speed of size reduction stays the same as it would have been on the surface, it will now take the smaller bubble 14 minutes to be eliminated. Compare this with the 10 times increase of elimination of bubbles when breathing oxygen compared to air.

Thus one may elect to recompress a patient to give instant relief, or have the patient breathe oxygen to speed up gas elimination. Coupling the two together however is the best of both worlds.

There are two shapes of bubbles, cylindrical and spherical. If one increases the pressure by two on a cylindrical bubble, the length is reduced by half, however to reduce the diameter of a sphere bubble by half the pressure needs to be increased by ten times.

Speed of bubble formation

From studies it was found that bubble formation is in some cases related to bottom depth and ascent speed. When ascent speed was normal but supersaturation threshold was exceeded, bubbles formed in around one to five minutes for severe DCS (and deeper exposure) and around 15 minutes for milder DCS.

The onset of symptoms after bubble formation also seemed to be depth linked, with deeper exposures having an onset of symptoms after bubble formation of around two minutes and shallower exposures around 10 minutes to two hours.

Silent bubbles and necrosis

It is thought that intravascular gas bubbles that are asymptomatic may have hidden effects such as aseptic necrosis and changes in the blood-brain barrier perfusion (altered blood flow to the brain). Note, caffeine constricts cerebral blood vessels that in turn reduce cerebral blood flow and can trap silent bubbles.

Bubble detection

Bubbles that enter the venous blood are carried to the heart where an ultrasound can detect them. The amount of bubbles detected is graded on different scales. It is thought that Doppler grade three and four have about 5% of inert gas in bubble form while the rest is dissolved.

Where do the bubbles go?

The venous blood is carried to the lungs where bubbles if large enough are trapped and filtered by the pulmonary circulation. If the bubble quantity increases (above Doppler grade three or four), then pulmonary artery pressures can rise to the level that bubbles are forced through the pulmonary filter and into the arterial blood.

The bubbles in the arterial blood from the lungs may enter the brain or spinal column. If bubble levels increase further, not enough blood will reach the lungs and the lungs can become choked (called the chokes), and breathing becomes difficult. At higher levels, it is possible that the bubbles will displace blood from the heart, leading to a heart attack and possible death. Bubbles may also enter the arterial side due to a PFO or ASD.

PFO

Approximately one in five people (20%) have a PFO (patent foramen ovale) or a hole in the heart. All people are born with this hole in the heart and in most cases a flap overlays this hole in about 24 hours after birth and seals the hole.

Anton Swanepoel

However, in some people the hole is not completely sealed, and blood can shunt from one side of the heart to the other. Bubbles coming from the compartments can bypass the lungs and enter the bloodstream on the way to the brain. The hole can be closed with surgery and return to diving is normally within 12 weeks.

ASD

ASD (atrial septal defect) is a form of congenital heart defect. The right and left atria are divided by an internal septum tissue, which if defective or missing could cause blood to travel from the left side of the heart to the right side of the heart, or vice versa. This can have the same effect as a PFO.

Pulmonary barotrauma and bubbles

If the internal pressure in the lungs compared to the ambient pressure exceeds 80 mm Hg (equivalent to around 2 to 3 ft water pressure), the lungs may be damaged and gas bubbles can be forced directly into the arterial side. This can be from holding one's breath when there is a pressure change (ascending) to ascending so fast that normal exhaling is not fast enough (run away ascent).

Repetitive dive and bubbles

Bubbles that are trapped in the lungs may be compressed on a second dive, including yo yo or sawtooth diving. These bubbles may then be compressed small enough to pass through the pulmonary filter and enter the arterial blood. If the pressure is reduced too fast, these bubbles may increase to their original size and possibly lead to DCS depending on their position in the body when they increase in size.

Note that it takes about a minute for blood to circulate the body and that the first organs after the lungs are the brain and spinal column.

It has been noted that a sudden shower of bubbles often occurs after a dive at the onset of movement when subjects are asked to move a limb. From observation in tests it was noted that showers of bubbles entered the inferior vena cava (IVC, vein carrying blood from the lower half of the body into the heart) during the compression (descent) part of a repetitive dive. The amount of bubbles entering the IVC can be increased on descent if the diver exercises (such as swimming down or swimming against a current) while descending on a repetitive dive.

Thus although repetitive dives may lessen the risk of DCS if done correctly (possibly due to elimination of nuclei), if done incorrectly they can increase the risk of DCS and severity of symptoms above that of a single dive even if the dive time for the single dive is equal to the dive time of the repetitive dives combined (for instance, one dive for 60 minutes compared to two or more dives with combined bottom time of 60 minutes, all to the same depth).

Valsalva and bubbles

Due to the Valsalva technique being widely used in diving, it should be pointed out the possible effects this technique can have on bubble formation, especially during decompression (possibly due to large swells passing over the diver requiring constant ear equalizing).

When performing a Valsalva maneuver it exerts pressure across the heart (around 40 to 60 mm Hg above ambient) and blood flow is decreased in the spinal cord venous side (drainage). With the spinal cord consisting of large fatty tissue with slow blood flow, reduction in the blood flow may promote bubble growth. A venous infarction mechanism may also occur (blockage of blood circulation that can lead to tissue death). In addition Valsalva also promotes transpulmonary passage of bubbles (bubbles passing through the lungs from the venous to arterial side) and blood shunting in people with PFO or ASD.

Anton Swanepoel

Mechanical heart valves and bubbles

Microbubbles form due to local high-pressure gradients at the level of the valve leaflets (known as cavitation) in mechanical heart valves. It was shown that cognitive impairments (decrease in working memory performance) occur due to persistent microbubble generation by mechanical heart valves that do not occur with biological valves. Considerable engineering is done to develop mechanical valves that do not create microbubbles.

However, for the diving person with a mechanical heart valve, the additional creation of microbubbles greatly increases the risk of DCS for not only does it create microbubbles, it may also increase the size of bubbles already in the system.

Body's reaction to bubbles

Due to bubbles being a foreign body, they have a biochemical effect on the blood and tissues. The body sees the bubbles as invaders and attacks the bubbles. The bubbles may disrupt and damage cells, that in turn can release proteins. Some of the proteins are vasoactive such as bradykinin, plasma complement, histamine (which increases vascular permeability), prostaglandin, and 5 hydroxytryptamine. 5 hydroxytryptamine trigger polymorphonuclear leukocytes (PMNs) that in turn stimulate cells to release histamine.

PMNs augment tissue damage by releasing cytotoxic substances, such as active oxygen metabolites and arachidonic acid (a polyunsaturated omega-6 fatty acid) that increase DCS risk.

In tests, rabbits were made resistant to DCS by decomplementing them of these proteins (using a drug made from cobra venom).

The rabbits were taken to 2 ata for ½ hour and made to run on a treadmill for one minute followed by a five minute rest. The rabbits were then returned to 1 ata and observed for symptoms. This procedure was repeated three times. All the rabbits experienced DCS symptoms in the first and second test (rabbits were immediately recompressed on first symptoms noticed and successfully treated).

On the last test, half of the rabbits were decomplimented. In this test none of the decomplimented rabbits experienced DCS symptoms yet all the other un-decomplimented rabbits experienced DCS symptoms, the same as they did in the previous tests.

Since the activation sensitivity of these proteins differs from person to person, it helps to explain the difference in individual DCS susceptibility. It is thought that the biochemical reaction to the bubbles may be more important than the mechanical effects of the bubbles, such as the size of the bubbles.

Human test on complement activation

To test the theory that the body's own reaction to bubbles enhances the risk of DCS, a number of tests were conducted. Blood was taken from 15 male subjects and subjected to a bubble test. Air bubbles were added to the blood that was then left to stand for ½ hour. If there was a large activation of protein blood complement then the person was deemed more susceptible to DCS.

To then test the theory further the subjects deemed less susceptible was subjected to more provocative dive profiles than the more susceptible subjects. The less susceptible subjects had far higher bubble scores (average bubble grade 3.1 against 2.8), yet no DCS incidences were reported compared to 45% DCS incidence in the more susceptible subjects even though they had a less provocative dive profile.

Anton Swanepoel

It is then seen that the sensitivity of blood protein complimentary activation plays a major role in individual DCS susceptibility.

-Acclimation

Due to the bubbles activating the protein compliments which get fragmented on activation, causing the proteins to be depleted in the process and need to be replaced. This replacement takes time and is seen as the adaption period (not to be confused with the around seven day adaption period of nuclei crushing and regeneration). The rabbit test mentioned before was the proof that DCS susceptibility could be altered by altering the protein complement.

-De acclimation

From further tests done on the rabbits and on tests done on humans it was found that two days after exposure to pressure was stopped (diving stopped) the individual (rabbit and human) was around twice as susceptible (for blood compliment activation) as before any exposure, and five days after stopping exposure the susceptibility was up to four times that of before first exposure. How long the individual takes to return to pre exposure susceptibility is not known. Thus on multiday diving, the individual can be more susceptible to DCS after a day to three days (depending on the individual's ability to replace proteins) of non-diving than if diving was continued daily.

-DSC susceptibility test

Humans can be tested for susceptibility to DCS before any pressure exposure by using blood plasma from the individual and exposing it to bubbles under controlled conditions and noting the sensitivity to complement activation.

-Conclusion on complement activation

The compliment susceptibility explains to a large degree (including individual nuclei creation) the large range of DCS susceptibility between people.

It also explains to a degree why some people may get DCS with very few or no visible bubbles, while others fizz like pop drink and do not get DCS.

Another question may be asked, as these are proteins that are activated, what role does eating habits play in the level and activity sensitivity of the proteins?

Blood clotting response

Microbubbles affect blood clotting due to activating coagulation (bubble surface acting as a foreign substance) and inducing platelet aggregation resulting in a clot forming at the bubble proximity.

The clot leads to fibrinolysis (a process that prevents blood clots from growing and becoming problematic) and local reaction to the thrombus. The microbubbles also adsorb macromolecules at the gas-blood interface that provokes molecular conformational changes (such as unfolding) that exposes regions of proteins that trigger blood coagulation.

Platelets adhere to bubble surfaces with the bubbles acting as platelet agonists with respect to aggregation. Microbubble induced endothelial damage causes tissue factor expression and subsequent platelet activation and thrombus generation. Platelets accumulate around air bubbles in the blood due to cellular reaction and as a result of the physicochemical flotation process. When the blood vessels become plugged, thrombus causes hypoxic local damage and tissue death.

Undetected and silent bubbles

Very little is known about the effects of small air emboli in the venous or arterial circulation. Bubbles may be clinically silent, however as yet undetected changes and damage may occur.

Anton Swanepoel

From a study on the Blackpool tables (used in tunnel and caisson work) it was found that many of the profiles produced bubbles that are barely detectable by current Doppler devices and that a significant number of miners would have bubbles that are not detectable. It is predicted that these bubbles would last for days as the bubbles are due to slow tissues.

Constant exposure to venous gas embolism has been shown to have a long term impact on the body even if bubbles are not detectable on a Doppler device. The changes may be long term that slowly manifest and could manifest as a problem later that one may not suspect to be diving related.

Mechanical tissue damage due to bubbles

A micro bubble traveling down the blood stream will continue to do so until it is caught by the lungs or lodges in the microcirculation. In the travel, the bubble may be compressed against the endothelial capillary wall that in turn causes a stripping away of endothelial cells and also an increase of large-pore radii. This may lead to intravascular fluids pouring out into the surrounding tissue and possible interstitial edema.

Bubbles also increase the hydrostatic pressure upstream to the bubble that causes additional fluid to pass into the interstitium (the space between cells in a tissue) and downstream from an obstructing bubble tissue, ischemia (insufficient supply of blood) and possibly tissue death due to hypoxia.

Inflammatory Response

Neutrophils (white blood cells) aggregate around the bubble to produce clumps and a local destructive process starts to form (thought to possibly be due to superoxide and hydroxyl radical production and proteolytic enzyme release).

Membrane permeability is increased that leads to fluids and protein leaking that in turn facilitate interstitial pulmonary edema. Bubble size plays a major role and the process normally starts as the circulating bubble is trapped in a small arteriole or capillary (100 to 1000 μm).

Stirring and transient effects on bubbles

Stirring is a term that relates to the effect of blood moving past a bubble or the elimination of gas from a tissue. Stirring does not affect small bubbles much, but does affect the gas concentration in the surroundings of the bubble.

Transient relates to the gas that moves to the immediate surroundings of a new bubble, or a bubble that moves to a new location, this could be important for the formation of a bubble from nuclei, however it does not affect later size changes of the bubble.

Transport and bubbles

Transporting a patient with suspected DCS in certain helicopters and fixed wing aircraft is thought to possibly increase bubble formation. The theory is that the vibration of the aircraft may cause bubbles to form or grow. It is thus suggested that the patient be put in an area with the least amount of vibration and if possible on an insulated mattress.

The cabin pressure maintained may also be a problem as few aircraft are able to maintain a sea level pressure. Even commercial aircraft have a reduced cabin pressure. A reduced ambient pressure may cause bubbles to grow further and additional bubbles to form.

Anton Swanepoel

It may be possible for the aircraft to fly at a reduced altitude, however this may not always be possible, and even if possible, it adds to the risk of crashing, including added fuel usage (sometimes up to 30%), and potentially slows the aircraft down while also stresses the aircraft due to increased wind resistance.

Intrapulmonary arteriovenous shunt (IPAV)

We normally think that blood leaving the right ventricle passes through the pulmonary microcirculation via capillaries and then returns to the left heart via the pulmonary veins. However, it has been shown that anatomical arteriovenous anastomoses exist in the lung (a union between the venous and arterial side) and allows blood to shunt from the venous side to the arterial side, bypassing the lung filters. The diameters of these vessels are in the order of up to 55 µm (0.055 mm) in infants and 200 µm (0.2 mm) in adults.

These connections may allow bubbles to pass from the venous side to the arterial side of the lungs where they can increase the risk of DCS. Exercise is seen to increase the amount of shunting due to increasing blood pressure. From tests done by Wilkinson and Fagan on fresh lungs in infants after sudden death it was noted that very low pressure (<7.5 mm Hg, <3.68 psi) was needed to cause shunting.

A study done by the Department of Human Physiology, University of Oregon, found that breathing oxygen for one minute reduced shunting, and breathing oxygen for two minutes eliminated shunting, however shunting promptly resumed upon breathing air. Divers should thus be aware that shunting will resume on the surface when air is breathed again so are urged to stay a few minutes longer on the highest O2 deco mix on the surface and take it easy when exiting the water (leave deco tanks in the water for later retrieval, or hand them off).

The reason oxygen breathing reduces or eliminates shunting is thought that alveolar hyperoxia prevents blood flow through arteriovenous shunt pathways. This may be due to vasoconstriction due to hyperoxia as seen in hyperbaric oxygen treatment (HBO).

In another study it was found that hypoxia induces the opening of IPAV shunts and may be a reverse of hyperoxia, thus the systemic vessels may vasodilate in response to hypoxia and increase shunting.

The number of bubbles and bubble dissolving speed
The speed that a bubble shrinks and dissolves is related to the number of bubbles forming in a local site in a tissue.

The more bubbles form together, the faster they will deplete excess dissolved inert gas in the local tissue, thus the bubbles will not grow as large as a single or fewer bubbles would have grown. This in turn will cause the inert partial pressure in the tissue to drop faster as the gas dissolves into the bubbles. Due to the tissue inert gas pressure dropping faster the gas pressure in the bubble will reach supersaturation sooner compared to the tissue gas pressure, allowing gas from the bubble to diffuse back into the tissue sooner and be taken away by the blood. This allows multiple bubbles to shrink and dissolve faster than a single bubble.

Smaller bubbles may also exact less damage to artery walls and local tissue and could allow some blood to pass helping to prevent necrosis that a single or few larger bubbles may create due to total blood flow blockage.

CO2 and bubbles

In experiments with rabbits it was found that the percentage of CO_2 in the bubbles tended to decrease at first and then increase with post-decompression time, and that CO_2 may play a role in the initiation and early growth of bubbles. The total dynamics is not yet fully understood.

Bubbles in blood

Although surface tension, blood pressure, and inherent unsaturation promote diffusion of gases out of bubbles in the bloodstream, stabilizers may allow small bubbles to exist even with a negative pressure in the bubble compared to its surroundings.

Non rigid stabilized bubbles can change size as they move through the circulatory system such as in small pulmonary vessels and allow bubbles to possibly enlarge due to a lower blood pressure. If there is no inherent unsaturation, O_2 and N_2 in the lungs diffuse into the bubbles; these gases may diffuse out of the bubble again in the systemic circulation into a tissue or possibly other bubbles, unless the bubble reached a critical size and starts to grow.

Chapter 15

What is decompression sickness?

Asking a certified diver about what DCS is, you will most probably get a very exact and text book answer. However, ask the top people in the field of decompression research and it is more a, well we think this is what happens but it is not totally true all the time thus we do not have the full understanding yet. Note that DCS is not actually defined and agreed upon by the medical community.

One of the problems of defining decompression sickness is its varied symptoms, thus decompression sickness is often used to classify symptoms rather than the actual cause. The same symptom could have been manifested from another cause, such as a headache from dehydration or joint pain due to overworking a muscle. If all aches and pains are symptoms of DCS then most old people have DCS. There is also the problem of people that violated so or so rule (may have skipped a safety stop) and believe that they are bent, often manifesting symptoms (even vague neurological symptoms).

First DCS report

The French were the first to use compressed air to push water out of tunnels in the early 1640s and allow the workers to work deeper. Consequently the first case of decompression sickness was reported in 1641 by Triger, although the term 'bends' was only coined at the building of the Brooklyn bridge (started in 1869 and took 14 years to complete).

Bubble relationship and DCS

The relationship between bubbles and DCS incidence is not totally understood.

Anton Swanepoel

Divers without bubbles get DCS, divers with high bubble scores do not get DCS, and some in the middle get either DCS or not, it's a crap shoot.

DCS is normally associated with joint and muscle pain, but may result in unconsciousness of the diver, paralysis, weakness, tiredness, tingling, unable to urinate, difficulty breathing, and death (there are cases in which bubbles have been found in a diver who died more than a month after a dive). In some cases a diver may have what is called decompression stress, here the diver may only be excessively tired and thirsty without any joint or muscle pain.

The diver does not have full DCS yet, but is on the verge, the body is trying its best to cope with an excess of bubbles in the system. The symptoms normally resolve after some hours if not provoked by exercise or warm baths and showers where it is possible to excite bubbles, causing full DCS with pain. When this happens recompression will most probably be the only way to resolve the symptoms.

Risk of CNS DCS seems to be the greatest in deep bounce dives (dives with short bottom times and relatively deep), and is often done by recreational divers wishing to go deep but not exceed no decompression times.

Factors that increase risk of DCS
In cold water vasoconstriction and blood redistribution can affect inert gas diffusion rates, however staying still in cold water will greatly reduce whole body inert gas exchange, while exercising in cold water will increase whole body inert gas exchange.

Any condition that affects blood flow to the tissues will affect inert gas diffusion rates and exchange (increasing DCS risk if lowered blood flow). Conditions that will increase perfusion can lower DCS risk on decompression, including hypoxia, carbon dioxide inhalation, a supine body position, any vasodilators and negative pressure breathing (using a regulator that is hard to breathe from or a CCR with low loop volume or inefficient design so as to cause restricted breathing).

Factors that increase gas exchange at depth increase DCS risk, while factors that increase gas exchange at decompression stops reduce DCS risk. Thus DCS risk will be decreased if divers are cold at the bottom and warm and immersed during decompression (not using dry chambers) or being supine if decompressing in a dry chamber.

Smoking
Smoking causes blood vessel damage due to nicotine and fat deposits, including enhanced thrombosis that is seen to be conducive to bubble formation. Lung damage from smoking may also lead to increased pulmonary bubble shunts and possible increased risk to arterial gas embolism. It is also thought that the CO in the blood of smokers (can reach levels of around 10%) can increase the risk of DCS and increase symptoms in DCS.

Foreign objects
Just for interest, swallowing a foreign object can puncture your lungs and cause an air embolism. A 2009 medical report was done on a 59-year-old woman who was treated for an air embolism after swallowing a fish bone. The fish bone punctured the lung and allowed gas to escape out of the lung. So watch out when eating sushi on your deco stops. ☺ More seriously, if you accidentally bite a piece off from your mouthpiece, then do not swallow it, spit it out.

Anton Swanepoel

Gasses affecting bubble filtering

It was concluded from tests on dogs that halothane (a general anesthetic) interferes with the capacity of the lungs to filter air from the pulmonary circulation.

Although it will be unlikely that you would have an operation requiring general anesthesia directly after a deep decompression dive, the question is what other gasses and chemicals interfere with the lungs' ability to filter bubbles that may be breathed before, during and after decompression?

The US navy reported (Naval Medical Research and Development Command report number NMRI- 92- 33) that it found toluene of 136 ppm surface equivalent contamination from air supply hoses making them unfit for use. Toluene is a solvent that is sometimes used as an inhalant drug due to its intoxicating properties, however when inhaling toluene it has the potential to cause severe neurological harm.

Helium and DCS

From the gas properties of Helium gas it is thought that Helium needs a greater supersaturated partial pressure for bubbles to form than from Nitrogen gas. However, from studies on 1400 rats on Helium and Nitrogen saturation it was found that Helium needed around 9 to 11% less supersaturated partial pressure to form bubbles, making ascent speed critical. Due to this, tri-mix can have a higher DCS risk than air as nitrogen is more forgiving when it comes to fast ascents. Interestingly however, it was noted that tri-mix also had a higher DCS risk than heliox. Clearly gasses in the body behave differently than our understanding of them out of the body and Helium does not like to follow the ideal gas laws.

Alcohol and DCS risk

Apart from being drunk and making mistakes that can lead to DCS (incorrect ascent rates and omitted decompression) there are long-term changes in the body with alcohol use. Alcohol is the only drug that permanently changes a person's DNA over time.

Alcohol primarily affects the central nervous system by influencing neurotransmission to produce intoxication, in addition to changing gene expression in the brain. There are around 50 000 different genes in our cells, however only a number of them are turned on in each one of us, resulting in giving us unique eyes, skin, hair and personality, called gene expression.

Alcohol activates different genes and may switch off already active genes, resulting in changes in mood, behavior, thinking, brain damage, learning, memory, neuron functions, neuropeptide signaling (modulating nerve cell activity), myelin structure (needed for communication between nerve cells) and premature aging. From current research it was found that more than 300 genes get activated by alcohol consumption over time. The changes also result in a greater addiction to alcohol with increased physical dependence and craving for it, in addition to giving you a greater reward feeling when consuming alcohol or a greater withdrawal crash when you refrain from drinking alcohol. The longer and in greater amounts you consume alcohol the more dependent you become to it and the harder it is to stop.

Excessive alcohol consumption causes liver dysfunction (possibly permanent damage) that can predispose the diver to DCS. There is also speculation that alcohol consumption changes blood surface tension and inherent gas uptake and release in tissues. In a study done on Japanese divers, a positive connection between alcohol consumption and DCS risk was made.

Anton Swanepoel

The role of fat in decompression and DCS

The role of fat on both decompression and DCS is not totally clear or understood as it is quite complex. The thought is that being overweight can predispose you to DCS, but the link is not very strong or clear.

Fat is mostly seen as a passive tissue as its blood flow is controlled by arterial pressure. During exercise, blood flow to fat can increase four fold (10 ml to 40 ml/minute per 100 gram tissue) in addition to fat having a fivefold greater inert gas solubility than muscle.

Thus during exercise fat may hold more inert gas than muscle. Exercise can then also greatly increase the off-gassing of inert gas from fat, however during cold conditions, blood flow to fat is greatly reduced.

It is then a matter of timing that determines the role of fat in DCS risk. If an overweight diver is cold but does not exercise, the fat may have less inert gas loading than a similar weighted diver with more muscle as more blood flow will be going to the muscles. Thus the muscular diver may be more at risk than the less toned diver. If however the less toned diver is unfit and needs to exercise to keep up, blood flow will be greatly increased to fat tissue (while still being cold). The amount of inert gas that is then in the body of the less toned diver may then be substantially larger than the toned diver as the fat will hold more gas than muscle.

Were both to ascend and the less toned diver stops exercising (hanging on the mooring line or deco station) the blood flow to the fat will again be greatly reduced. With the additional inert gas in the fat, it will take the less toned diver longer to eliminate all the inert gas, making the diver more at risk of DCS. If you are un-toned, be fit. ☺

DCS symptom onset

Although DCS symptoms can occur hours later, it should be noted that around 66% of spinal DCS and 87% of cerebral DCS symptoms occur within 10 minutes of decompression. Muscular or pain only bends normally take longer, thus the faster the onset of symptoms the more dangerous the bends and the more likely residual damage may affect the diver after treatment. It is very important then to place the person on supplemental oxygen as soon as possible. Note that in some cases limb pain may precede spinal column DCS symptoms.

Although neurological DCS has a rapid symptom onset that can prove fatal, it can take time, painful time. Bauer reported in 1870 on a 35-year-old male caisson worker that died five days after incurring spinal cord DCS. Van Rensenlaer in 1891 published a report 'The pathology of caisson disease' on 25 post mortem examinations and included a case where the victim survived for 36 days. Sharples reported on a case of neurological DCS where the person died 38 days after the onset of DCS. In all cases it was found that the white matter in the spinal cord was affected rather than the gray matter and that there was destruction in the nerve tissues.

It is unlikely to have 100% recovery in all cases especially if symptoms occur fast after decompression, and even more so if treatment is delayed - prompt oxygen breathing and recompression is key to a full recovery.

DCS symptoms and profile

Neurological DCS is more common in divers than in tunnel workers where limb pain dominates and is thought to be due to rapid decompression from increased pressure with short durations as in bounce diving. It was found that such profiles create more CNS DCS than longer exposures to lower pressures. It is thus recommended that the ascent near the surface (last 30 ft)

Anton Swanepoel

be slow and that a safety stop should be made (recreational diving) before surfacing to reduce the incidence of CNS DCS in deep air bounce dives.

Breathing gas and DCS

From comparison of dive data from Thallman on US heliox diving against research with sheep on air dives, it seems that heliox deep bounce diving gives some protection to DCS over deep air bounce diving. This may be due to different tissue responses from the different breathing gasses even when on the same profile.

With deep air dives, as the depth increased, there was an increase in the percentage of CNS DCS compared to limb DCS, while on heliox there seemed no increase to the number of CNS DCS to limb DCS if the dives got deeper (although Thallman's own research did not show this).

This may be due to the large amount of fatty tissue in the spinal column (nitrogen has around five times the solubility in fat than water). Thallman did however find evidence to support a greater amount of Type II DCS (about twice) on Helium dives than air and could have been due to ascent rates.

Exiting the water after a dive

On exit, a diver is at increased risk of DCS due to a number of reasons. The diver is subjected to a sudden drop in pressure as the diver ascends from the last stop to the surface including a sudden drop of inspired oxygen partial pressure.

Divers are urged to breathe their highest deco mix for five to 10 minutes on the surface if possible before exiting the water. Divers are also subjected to increased physical exertion as the diver goes from in water weight to out of water weight. Gear suddenly becomes heavy and it is suggested that divers leave stages at the exit or hand them off if possible before exiting to reduce weight.

It should also be noted that there is a blood shift that occurs when one leaves the water and now enters a world of gravity again, the reverse of the immersion effect. Together these sudden changes may serve as a trigger point for DCS.

Oxygen DCS

Oxygen starts to behave as an inert gas and can produce oxygen DCS, normally at a PPO2 of 2 ata and over, although sometimes seen at pressures below 1.7 ata. For high partial pressures of O2, O2 bubbles can form at deeper depths, however symptoms are normally only seen after dives with very long decompression stops on pure O2 or close to pure O2, probably due to few people exceeding a 1.6 ata PPO2 in diving nowadays.

Symptoms normally include severe acute joint pain that manifest within minutes after surfacing. The symptoms normally disappear relatively quickly by themselves and are thought to be due to oxygen-filled bubbles. The bubbles are thought to be quickly absorbed into the surrounding tissue, lessening the pressure on pain receptors that results in a disappearance of the symptoms.

In a test done by the US Naval Medical Institute on dive profiles from 3112 dives, it was found that both a high PO2 and a high fraction of O2 contribute to DCS. When they created a new model that included an O2 compartment to tract O2 diffusion, a significant improvement in DCS prediction was found.

From animal experiments on high partial pressures of oxygen (2 ata and higher) it was seen that N2 increased the risk of DCS if used with high pressures of O2. Goats were subjected to a PPO2 of 3.5 ata + PPN2 of 2 ata, this created a greater DCS incidence than if the PPO2 was 3.5 ata with PPN2 lowered or with 2 ata PPN2 and a lower PPO2.

Later experiments found that O2 was around 88% as potent as N2 for serious DCS symptoms and around 38% as potent for fatal DCS. Thus at higher PPO2, oxygen bends are a real concern and may explain partly why deep air diving has a higher DCS risk than Helium diving. However, at altitude oxygen is far less potent than N2. In human tests, of 477 dives it was found that an increase of 1 ata inspired O2 had the same DCS risk as an inspired N2 increase of 0.4 ata.

Time to treatment and symptom resolution

Although hyperbaric oxygen treatment (HBO) is standard in treating decompression illness (DCI), there is conflicting thought as to the part the time from surfacing to treatment plays in the resolution of symptoms. HBO was first documented in 1662 and the first hyperbaric chamber (domicilium) was built by Henshaw.

Due to the risk of oxygen toxicity and fire, the first chambers used air for decompression. Drager was the first to explore oxygen use in chambers for DCS. His protocols were later put into practice in the late 1930s by Behnke and Shaw.

In a study done by Dr Werner Stipp (North Sea Medical Centre) it was shown that early HBO treatment for neurological DCI is robustly associated with a better outcome and that if treatment is delayed for 350 minutes (approximately six hours) after surfacing then HBO treatment is less effective and can result in residual symptoms and permanent damage.

It was also found that if oxygen is administered before HBO then an improvement in symptom resolution is seen with HBO treatment, and that delay in HBO treatment has less of an effect, kind of like a protection for a delay in treatment.

Chapter 16

Relation between bubbles and DCS

If all bubbles lead to DCS, then all fizzy drinks are bent. ☺

One of the big debates in decompression and DCS is the role bubbles play in the manifestation of DCS. It is theorized that bubbles are one of the leading causes of DCS, thus one would assume that the more bubbles the higher the incidence of DCS. However, it has been found that a bubble score of four on the Spencer scale does not always lead to DCS, and a score of one is not a guarantee of no DCS. In fact, there have been cases reported in tests where individuals got DCS with no bubbles detected.

The reason for the results is unclear, for it may be due to a lack of relationship between bubbles and DCS, or it may be due to operator error such as sampling errors or incorrect classification of bubble scores, time of testing (test directly after a dive and no bubbles may be present, but one hour later loads of bubbles may be present), stationary bubbles, and unknown parameters.

Another problem with Doppler bubble detection is that bubbles cannot always be seen and the tester needs to listen to the sound of bubbles. Noise from other sources may interfere as to the tester's own expectancy of the result (if a tester knew the subject made a dive profile commonly thought to result in DCS the tester may be biased towards a higher bubble score). The problem of result expectancy may be overcome by recording the Doppler sounds and then give only the recordings to testers without any knowledge of the actual dive profile done.

In a test done by the US Navy in the mid 1970s to test deep stops, no significant difference in Doppler bubble scores for those developing DSC and those that did not develop DCS in the group was noted.

Anton Swanepoel

No divers in the deep stop group developed DCS, and their bubble scores were also lower. However, divers in a decompression schedule longer than the control group (more deco) with no deep stops also had no incidence of DCS, while their bubble score count was not significantly different than the ones in the control group that did get DCS.

Thus both longer deco and deep stop groups had no DCS, but only the deep stop group had a lower bubble count. This is another case for the argument that just because divers use a model and do not get bent does not mean the model is correct, for they can have a large amount of bubbles without knowing it and not get bent, and the original tissue loading model could have created the same results by adding more deco.

Although it is relatively easy to study and detect intravascular bubbles (that are linked to DCS), the formation of bubbles in extravascular tissue is unclear as to their role in DCS.

Data collected from 1986 dives for the Canadian forces shows that there is a tendency for divers to have more grade three and four bubble scores on helium dives, however they seem to be able to tolerate grade three and four helium dive bubbles more than an air dive grade three or four score. More divers are reported to get DCS on air decompression than Heliox decompression. This could be due to the helium's fast off-gassing rate that may allow the helium bubbles to shrink fast, however this is still unclear at the moment.

It should also be noted that high bubble scores need to be noted against the profile done, such as the depth and time of the dive, as this can affect the DCS risk for the same bubble score. Another point is the time of onset of the bubbles. A high score immediately after a dive (suggesting fast tissues) can give a different DCS risk compared to a high bubble score that only formed hours after the dive (suggesting slow tissues).

It is thought that when bubbles form, they are isolated from circulation and decrease the gradient between tissue and arterial blood inert gas tension, thus reducing the inert gas elimination rate.

The same bubble score for different dive profiles also has a different DCS risk. A bubble score of four for a deep decompression dive carrys in general a higher risk than a bubble score of four for a shallow recreational dive. This may be due to increased chance of bubbles forming on deep dives at ascent and more inert gas available for bubble growth on decompression dives.

Chapter 17

Testing

Before one can argue about deep stops, or even decompression, one needs to understand a bit more about the testing done and how that affects the results of the tests.

Thus before one can take a test result from experiments done and run away with a theory, one needs to understand that all experiments and tests have problems, limits, aims and protocols. In a number of the experiments it is possible that had a new parameter been introduced, the results would have been far different. Thus, even though results may be repeatable for one test, the same theory or conclusion may not hold for different circumstances. Tests done on 100 ft air dives and the conclusions made from the results may thus be totally different when the same theory is tested on a 300 ft tri-mix dive.

History of bubble testing

Robert Boyle was the first to detect bubbles in living organisms when he did experiments using a vacuum chamber, a bubble in a vipers eye in 1660 (good wine year) caught his eye. ☺

In 1774 Erasmus Darwin (an English physician) published results of tests he conducted to test the theory of vapor bubbles. Drawing around 113ml (4 ounces, UK) of blood from an assistant and placing it in a vacuum, bubbles were observed to form.

When Darwin redid the experiment with blood from a sheep without allowing it to get in contact with air (a blood filled jugular secured at both ends was removed from a sheep), no bubbles formed. It was then reasoned that the exposure to atmospheric air caused the bubbles to form and prevention of exposure to atmospheric air may prevent bubbles from forming.

Vacuum bubble theory is a large reason why astronauts pre-breathe oxygen before space flight to try and prevent bubbles from forming when pressure is reduced due to altitude.

Bubble tests and sharp shooting

One can make a comparison to sharp shooting with bubble and DCS testing. If one were to stand in front of a target and shoot at point blank range, one would most probably hit the target even with eyes closed. Thus the conclusion could be made that seeing the target is not that important.

Trying the same test at 100 ft would most probably result in the discovery that seeing the target is important, but that bullet drop was not so critical. At 1000 ft the realization would be made that bullet drop is critical for accurate shooting, and if the test was done on a windless day the results may exclude wind as a factor.

The same test done to 1000 ft on a very windy day would conclude that wind is a factor, as an unknown parameter was introduced that was not tested for in the first test. A test at 3000 ft range would suddenly see not only being able to see the target, wind and bullet drop, but also humidity, the spin of the earth, the heat of the barrel of the gun and the powder loading of each bullet (different batches of bullets may differ in powder type and amount) as important.

If one were then to think of including all the parameters of the long shot when making a short distance shot, you may end up with different results. Say for instance you see that on a strong windy day you need to aim 5 ft into the wind away from the target to make a hit on a 3000 ft shot and you make a 30 ft distance shot and apply the same principle from the long shot on a strong windy day, that you need to aim 5 ft into the wind away from the target, you are going to miss the bad guy and end up shooting the good guy, oops.

Anton Swanepoel

Thus, one needs to be careful in taking results from tests and making conclusions on dives whose profiles fall outside the scope of those tested or that has additional parameters not tested for.

Testing problems

Following are a number of problems that may be present on a test and could affect the results of the tests.

Control group

In order to test a theory conclusively, one needs a control group or results from tests already done with the same parameters. This is where control groups come in.

For medicine, a number of candidates are normally given a placebo without their knowledge, their results are then tested against the candidates who received the actual medicine.

In diving, candidates are given a set dive schedule and their results are compared to other candidates who used a different dive schedule with different stops and times. If the results favor the test group against the control group then the theory may be called correct. Testing with control groups is one of the biggest problems with the new bubble models, as there is little actual comparative testing done.

There are arguments that many technical divers use the models for deep technical dives with very little incidence of decompression sickness. Even though it is true, it is argued that the mere absence of decompression sickness reported is not proof that the theory is sound as one does not know what would not have worked or what would have worked better.

The diver may have done the dive on Bühlmann tables and also not have gotten decompression sickness. In addition, since there is no control, it is difficult to expand on the theory, meaning should stops be done deeper or shallower, for longer or shorter?

Bubble models are in many cases a desktop model that is built on many assumptions with very little actual testing against control groups with the exact same parameters, remember the shooting comparison.

Blinding

One of the problems with bubble scores is that the tester may be objective or biased. If the tester knows the dive profile, a higher bubble score may be given to those profiles the tester believes are at greater risk. By ensuring the tester does not know the profile, a recording of the bubble noise can be made and given to a tester removed from the testing facility. This way a greater degree of accuracy may be possible.

End point

Choosing an end point for any test is a big decision. In decompression profile testing it comes down to, is the test going to be conducted to the point that divers get DCS, or just until it is clear that bubble scores differ significantly. Testing for DCS as an end point is a very hard evidence way, however this is not always practical or desired.

Testing for bubbles as an end point is in most cases easier and more accepted. However, with the poor understanding of the relation between DCS and bubble scores, it creates an additional question against the validity of the test results and conclusions.

Number of subjects

The actual number of subjects tested is very important for any experiment. If one only tests one subject, then there is large room for error. The more subjects used in the test, the more the theory can be tested, for in diving as in many other things there are individuals who are resistant to DCS and there are others that are susceptible to DCS.

It is believed that old navy and deep saturation divers are normally more resistant to DCS and that individuals who have a history of DCS may be more susceptible to DCS.

Number of samples taken

If only one bubble sample is taken after a dive, it is not that accurate. It is accepted that in general bubble scores peak around 60 minutes after a dive. Testing before and after this window can give additional data on how bubbles formed. The more samples, the more data and the more solid the conclusions from the tests.

For interest, to get a 99% confidence that a profile is less than 1% risk, you need more than 468 clean dives in a row to prove that statistically, many tests do not have that amount of bulk dives.

If you do 10 dives in a row with no incidence, then you have a 95% confidence that your profile has less than around 31% risk. And that is only for the profile you tested, if the depth changes you have to retest for the new profile. Multilevel profiles (tables or computers) create multiple depth profiles that each needs to be tested.

Consistency

When conducting comparison tests, it is very important that there is consistency between test groups. Descent and ascent rates need to be the same (unless that is tested), bottom times and depths also need to be the same.

The temperature of the water and work done under water needs to be controlled, in addition to a number of other parameters to ensure accurate comparison.

Specificity

Specificity is the ability to identify an individual in a group with a specific condition correctly. Specificity and sensitivity are opposites when it comes to testing. As the one goes up, the other goes down. The reason is that to identify a condition in an individual, one has to define the condition by defining the symptoms that would produce that condition. This could lead to missing a number of individuals who have the condition due to not all symptoms being present even though the condition is.

Sensitivity

Sensitivity is the ability of a test to find all individuals in a group of a population with a specific condition being tested. For instance, to test for lung cancer, one test could be to remove the lungs of all the individuals in a group and note for lung cancer, this will be highly accurate, although not really practical. ☺

Rest period

The rest period between test dives is very important. If the test period is too short, there will still be a significant amount of residual nitrogen in the tissues which can possibly affect the results of the following dive. The next dive would then in essence be a repetitive dive and not a new dive. The deeper and longer the first dive was for, including the amount of decompression done, will affect the amount of residual gas in the diver's body after ascending from the dive. Normal rest periods used in tests are from four to seven days.

False positives

False positives are when a diagnosis of DCS is made, and the actual cause is not DCS (for the purpose of DCS testing). This may be due to incorrectly interpreting symptoms and signs or the individual being tested manifesting symptoms due to a belief on the part of the individual of being bent, sometimes seen when individuals are given a placebo and believe they are given medicine, the individual then recovers without the help of medicine. One needs to view results of high DCS with caution if false positives have not been accounted for.

False negatives

False negatives are when a diagnosis is made that the symptoms and signs are due to some other malady than DCS when it is in fact due to DCS (for the purpose of DCS testing). This may be due to incorrectly interpreting symptoms and signs, or due to the individual being tested not mentioning symptoms or believing that those symptoms are not related to DCS. This is sometimes seen in the denial group that refuses to admit they are bent even when they violated many known rules for decompression. Results with low incidence of DCS need to be viewed with caution if false negatives have not been accounted for as the true number may be far greater. This is difficult to do without a control group.

Wet or dry testing

There is a marked difference when testing is done in a wet or dry environment. Tests were done with two schedules; one a 66 ft (20 m) for 70 minutes and another 178 ft (54 m) for 20 minutes. The tests were first done in a wet chamber and repeated the following week in a dry chamber.

From the tests it was noted that cardiac output and internal functions were reduced for up to two days after immersion in water. Bubble scores were also different and it was noted that decompression time was increased. This would make one wonder as to the long-term effect of diving on the heart and internal organs.

Noise

Any false positives or false negatives are seen as noise and dilute the data set. There will always be a certain percentage of the data that does not add value to the test and needs to be catered for, thus the larger the sample of data the less effect noise data will have on the results.

Way of measuring results

There are a number of different ways of measuring the results of a dive profile. Measurements can be done with a 2D Doppler device or with an ultrasound and a display where bubbles can actually be seen. The site of measurement is also important, whether the location for bubble detection is in the venous or arterial side and if it is near the heart or in tissues. The position and movement of test subjects also have an influence on results.

Expected results

It is possible that some test results may become skewed if the outcome of the test is a certain expectation, this can be due to measurements only taken that would favor the outcome desired or the actual test itself conducted in a way to favor the outcome desired. If you want to prove that sharks are not attracted to blood then do your tests in the dessert, no self-respecting shark will bite you. ☺

Repeatable results

The test results also need to be able to be repeatable and not be one-off effects. This is normally the theory behind double blind tests.

Range of the tests done

Often a test is done on a profile and the results and conclusions made based on that one profile. However the conclusions may be incorrect if the same test were done with a different profile. Different tissues M-values control different dive profiles, for a conclusion to be valid it needs to be tested over a range of different dive profiles and circumstances.

Validity of outcome

It was noted that many tables that fare good in chamber trials failed when used in actual diving. A study done in 1999 by the National Hyperbaric Centre found that gas uptake in the muscles can increase by a factor of three when light work is done at the bottom compared to resting at the bottom. Thus tests done where divers are resting may fail due to inadequate gas uptake in the test compared to real-world movement of divers in the water. If the diver has to work harder, such as fighting against a very strong current, then the gas uptake will be even higher in the muscles.

Chapter 18

Ascent speed

As if decompression algorithms and deep stops are not enough to argue about, we have ascent speed as well. ☺

There is much debate as to what is a safe ascent speed 10, 30, 60 or 100 ft/minute. In addition to if you should keep the speed the same on the whole dive or if you can ascend quicker from deeper depths. Even Prof. J.S. Haldane and physiologist Sir Leonard Hill disagreed on ascent speed. Haldane proposed a staged ascent where Hill proposed a uniform ascent (slow bleed ascent).

Staged Ascent

A staged ascent allows a diver to ascend at the fastest safe speed without undue risk of bubbles forming, while limiting additional on-gassing in slower tissues so as not to increase shallow decompression stops more than is needed. Time is then spent at each stop to give the leading tissue compartment time to reach a safe level before one resumes ascent until the same or another compartment reaches critical supersaturation.

Since the faster compartments are the first compartments to reach supersaturation and off-gas fast, the initial stop times are normally short and gradually the control shifts to slower and slower compartments while shallower stop times increase.

Slow bleed ascent

Hill's slow uniform ascent has prevailed in caisson and tunnel decompression and recently is being used in very deep diving (normally saturation diving). The slow bleed ascent in saturation diving normally only looks at one tissue due to the dive being so long and only the longest tissue affects calculation, thus you do not have multiple tissues but a continuum of tissues creating a smooth curve or straight but very slow ascent.

Anton Swanepoel

Ascent speed history

Although many people believe that the US Navy 60 ft/minute original ascent rate is based on many experiments and tests, it is not correct and was actually a disagreement compromise, see text later.

Although this speed was accepted by the US Navy and UK Navy in 1956 and incorporated in the 1958 US Navy air tables it was selected long before and noted in a book by Sir Robert Henry Davis (1870 – 1965), (Deep Diving and Submarine Operations, First edition, 1909).

In the 1950s the Experimental Diving Unit (EDU), then located on the Anacostia River in the Washington, D.C. Navy Yard, used a volume known as the Bureau of Ships Diving Manual as a reference (NAVSHIPS 250-880, issued in 1952). The volume stated a max ascent speed not to exceed 25 ft/minute.
25 ft/minute ascent speed was also reflected in the Submarine Medicine Practice at the time (NAVPERS 10838, issued in 1949).

La Plongée published in 1958 by the French naval Groupe d'Etudes et de Recherches Sous-Marines de la Marine Nationale (GERS) called for an ascent rate of 33 ft/minute for the last 33 ft (10m) of the dive, although the ascent from depth may be higher (up to 60 m or roughly 180 ft/minute for self-contained equipment).

In 1956 to 1957, Officer-in-Charge Maino des Granges and his team were working on the new air decompression tables (released in 1958). A hot debate arose between WR Doug Fane who represented the West-coast Underwater Demolition Team and hard-hat divers. Fane was adamant that 25 ft/minute was too slow for his frogmen and wanted 100 ft/minute or faster. Hard-hat divers were adamant that this speed would not be possible when hauling divers up in the current heavy dive gear with the winches they had.

Granges informed both sides that ascent speed is critical for decompression calculations and that creating two sets of tables would not be practical. The compromise, 60 ft/minute ascent rate, being the fastest rate a hard-hat diver could be physically hauled to the surface, and the fastest rate a free swimming diver could swim to the surface.

In the 1986 revision, Comex reduced the ascent rate for their air tables from 15 to 12 m/minute (around 50 ft down to 40 ft/minute) and in 1990 the French Navy reduced the ascent rate for their air tables from 18 to 12 m/minute (60 ft down to 40 ft/minute).

How fast do you think you are coming up?

Spencer Campbell did an experiment to see if recreational divers could correctly control a 60 ft/minute ascent rate. He took a group of sports divers to exactly 60 ft and let them ascend uncontrolled. The average ascent speed was around 170 ft/minute. When asked, all divers said that they thought they were coming up at 60 ft/minute. Clearly making a slow ascent by following your smallest bubble and making a slow ascent without the aid of a beeping dive computer is very hard to do.

Ascent speed and breath-hold diving

Native divers of Tuamotu Archipelago, Polynesia, have a malady called "Taravana", which is an acute decompression sickness due to rapid ascent from depths in excess of 165 ft (50 m) on breath-hold. The divers make short (around 30 to 50 second bottom time dives with around 100 second total dive time) dives to depths in excess of 165 ft (around 40 to 60 dives a day) to recover pearls.

Anton Swanepoel

Although Taravana symptoms are similar to DCS, being paralysis, visual changes, hearing loss, dizziness and death, some symptoms are not. Hypoxia is proposed as the cause as divers struggle to get oxygen into their lungs. Many divers end up with permanent brain and spinal cord injuries. This type of diving is seen to be where breath-hold diving can possibly cause decompression sickness.

A book about Tarvana called 'Breath-hold Diving and the Ama of Japan' edited by H. Rahn and T. Yokoyama was published in 1965 (publication number 1341 of the National Research Council, Washington, D.C).

Dr. Paulev, a Dane, took a submarine crew for training on submarine escape procedures in Bergen, Norway in the 1960s. Free divers would accompany the trainee submarine crew as they performed submarine escape ascent needed to qualify for naval submarine duty. The depth was 100 ft and Dr. Paulev did around 60 dives with around two minute bottom time, each followed by surface intervals of around 1-2 minutes. Dr. Paulev continued his dives and after around 5 hours of free diving he made his last dive, climbed out of the tank and collapsed as he walked away. He was promptly taken to a recompression facility and successfully treated.

As he was the medical officer on duty he wrote a report of the proceedings of the day, an article for the Journal of Applied Physiology was later written. This was the first time DCS was recorded in free diving.

Dr. Paulev investigated the incidence further and concluded that the short surface interval was not enough to allow nitrogen to off-gas between dives.

Dr. E. Lanphier did further studies on repeated breath-hold diving and calculated that if the surface interval equals the dive time then the nitrogen loading would be equal to 50% of the depth for the duration of both the dive time and surface interval.

For example if a diver did a 140 ft dive for two minutes followed by a two minute surface interval, then the nitrogen loading would be equal to a dive to 70 ft for four minutes (on rapid ascents the depth would be 65% of the bottom depth). A ratio of 2:1 for surface interval to bottom time reduces the depth to around 30% of the max breath-hold depth.

Breath-hold divers doing many repetitive dives over 100 ft are at great risk of developing DCS and so too breath-hold divers practicing for long durations (around three to five hours) even in shallower waters.

Interesting submarine procedures

When the navy learned that lung over expansion injuries due to breath-hold on submarine escape training was occurring, they took it very seriously; or the brass did but the crew at first not always as much. Ex submarine crew Charlie Christiansen recalls how they tried to come as high out of the water as possible. To try and prevent this, the navy installed stations along the way, sort of like a barrel with air in at depth.

Divers would be waiting at the stations and if a trainee was seen holding his breath on the way up the diver would grab the trainee and push him into the barrel where he got a stern talking to and let go. Sometimes they just got grabbed and punched in the stomach to make them exhale and let go. Topside they had to stand at attention while a medical examiner checked for any medical issues.

Charlie Christiansen

A device later used, called a 'Steinke hood' (named after its inventor, Lieutenant Harris Steinke) was a sort of life jacket that had relief valves in to allow expanding air in the jacket to be vented on ascent. This air was routed via two hoses into a hood going over the submarine escapee's head. The hood had a clear see-through sheet that allowed you to see (like a mask) and allowed the person to breathe and talk on ascent due to the air released from the expanding jacket. To make sure the trainees did not hold their breath (one could not be sure if the bubbles where from the jacket or trainees breathing) they had to sing (normally go ho ho ho) on the way up. Early Santa Clause practice. ☺

The Steinke hood replaced the Momsen lung and was later replaced by escape suits, called Submarine Escape Immersion Equipment.

Another interesting tale is that the fire fighting rebreathers used on the submarines could not be used for underwater operations or emergency escape as it contained a lithium hydroxide canister. The result of water mixing with the lithium hydroxide caused an explosive reaction, apparently very good for fishing though, early dynamite fishing. ☺

Ascent speed and bubbles

It is known that gas still dissolved in the tissues and gas that is free behave differently in addition to gas in free form negatively affecting off-gassing. Bubbles are thought to be initiated at micronuclei (gas-phase bubbles in blood and tissues) and that ascent rate plays a large role in the bubble size and behavior.

One may think that a slow ascent rate is best as it maintains the micronuclei under pressure and helps to prevent bubble formation. However, too slow ascent rates may prolong decompression as it slows inert gas diffusion and possibly causes additional inert gas uptake in slower compartments. It is then a tradeoff between optimum off-gassing or decompression time and risk of bubbles forming.

It has been demonstrated experimentally that for helium dives, deeper stops and slower ascent rates are needed to prevent bubble formation than air dives. Recent studies have shown that the growth rate of helium bubbles with equal concentration of helium and nitrogen in the tissues is six times greater for helium than nitrogen due to its greater diffusion rate.

From experiments done by Dr Valerie Flook it was found that slowing the ascent was beneficial in accordance to Doppler scores and that the slower ascents were more beneficial to the brain than stops (for no deco dives). However, if inserting a stop, the depth of the first stop made either a positive or negative impact depending on the bottom depth and time.

For shorter exposures the shallow stop is more beneficial than inserting a deep stop, and for longer exposures inserting a deep stop was more beneficial than a shallow stop. In Dr Flook's experiments she also found that bubbles form when a certain partial pressure gradient is exceeded, and that the partial pressure gradient does not differ between tissues at the time of bubble formation.

Ascending faster from deeper depths

Regardless of the ascent speed you choose for the shallow portion of the dive, the question is, can and should you keep it the same for your initial ascent?

The original theory was (and still is for some) to get out of the water as soon as possible. Thus, ascending at a faster speed from the bottom to your first stop was seen as limiting additional gas uptake.

It is also believed that the slow compartments (for compartment or tissue models) have not on-gassed as much and that the faster compartments can handle a higher pressure difference between the tissues and ambient pressure, thus one can ascend quicker on the deep portion of the dive. This method is mainly done by noncommercial technical divers who do bounce dives (dives with short bottom times, even 3 hours at 300 ft is short compared to deep multi week long bottom time saturation diving).

It is now believed that the initial ascent plays a large part in later bubble formation and that a fast initial ascent is not ideal. It is also thought that ascent speed should be slowed down the last 10 ft or so before a stop and that one should not ascend right up to the limit of a stop at the initial arrival of a stop, but to stay two to five ft below the stop for a portion of the stop. (Assuming using straight Haldanian or Bühlmann calculations with no Gradient Factor changes as this will already lower the critical supersaturation level).

For example, if the ascent rate chosen is 30 ft/minute and the first stop is at 120 ft, when the diver reaches 130 ft the ascent would be slowed to around 25ft/minute and the diver would stop at around 125 to 122 ft for about a minute if making a two minute stop. For the last part of the stop time the diver can move to the actual stop depth. This method is seen to keep the critical supersaturation just below the maximum value, just in case. Manually employing Gradient Factors maybe.

Interestingly saturation diving is seen as being safer than bounce dives, the decompression schedules are well tried and done in a dry chamber with more control with mostly access to medical personnel in emergencies.

Ascent speed and tables

Fixed dive tables are created with an intended ascent speed (mostly 33 ft/minute or 60 ft/minute). If your ascent speed does not match the speed that the table was designed for, your decompression schedule may be incorrect.

-Ascending faster than calculated

If you ascend at a rate faster than the table was calculated for, then you will reach your first stop sooner. Most tables (especially deep tri-mix and custom cut tables) calculate the off-gassing that occurs as you ascend.

By ascending faster, you will reach your stops with a higher dissolved gas supersaturation and you may exceed the critical pressure point and trigger bubbles to form or existing bubbles to grow too large by not having enough time to dissolve, one of the reasons deep stops were introduced.

These bubbles if not immediately causing problems could invalidate your decompression schedule as they will now require additional decompression to dissolve and shrink to a safe size and quantity.

-Ascending slower than calculated

Ascending slower than calculated by table designers will have you reach a stop with more dissolved gas in slow tissues, although faster tissues might have a lower value than calculated. The additional gas uptake can require more decompression than what was calculated by the table initially and also shift stops deeper than was initially calculated. The result may be that you miss decompression stops.

For instance, let's say the table is calculated at 30 ft/minute ascent rate and you ascend from 300 ft. If your first stop is at 210 ft, then it should take you three minutes to reach the stop. If you ascend at 15 ft/minute, then it would take you six minutes to reach 210 ft. Thus you will spend an additional three minutes below 210 ft, or if you average it, 1½ minutes additional at 255 ft. That is a substantial increase just for the bottom part even if you would speed up your ascent. If, however, you keep your ascent rate constant, then you can double the time from your bottom depth to your last stop.

For example, from 300 ft to 15 ft on a 30 ft/minute ascent it should take 9½ minutes to your last stop for ascent time (not counting stop or deco times).

If you then ascend at 15 ft/minute it would take an additional 9½ minutes or could be seen as about 4¼ minutes at 157.5 ft additional dive time (this is only an average for explanation purpose, the real on-gassing would be different).

The additional decompression you may need that was not calculated for is not the only problem, gas consumption will also be incorrect and one risks running out of breathing gas (especially in a gas sharing emergency where it is easy to not keep to calculated ascend speeds).

If you do want to ascend slower than the dive table was calculated for, then you need to add the additional travel time to your bottom time and recalculate your decompression.

Let's say for instance that you are diving to 120 ft for 15 minutes. The table ascent rate is 60 ft/minute, thus it will take you two minutes travel time, if you choose to ascend at 30 ft/minute, then it will take you four minutes. The additional two minutes are then added to your bottom time (now 17 minutes) and decompression if any is then recalculated.

Ascent speed and bubble size

Irrespective if bubbles in the system came from pre-existing bubble seeds or from dissolved gas coming out of the tissues or solution, a fast ascent speed does not help to keep the bubble volume small.

Smaller bubbles are more inclined to shrink during decompression, while larger bubbles are more inclined to grow, possibly leading to DCS. Bubbles can form due to direct excitation of critical micronuclei or by gradual bubble coalescing transitions, with ascent speed playing a major part in both.

Anton Swanepoel

Note that slower ascent tables (either hard or custom cut from software) are more sensitive to ascent speed variations. Thus if you have a table that was calculated for 30 ft/minute and you deviate 6 ft/minute (either fast or slow) it is a 20% deviation, where if you have a table calculated at 60 ft/minute and deviate by 6 ft/minute it is only a 10% deviation.

Slower ascents may help to control bubble formation, but are more sensitive to ascent deviation and you need to be far better with your buoyancy control if using slower ascent profiles.

Ascent speed and deep stops

Deep stops and slower ascent rates work together, slower ascent rates are akin to deep stops, helping to prevent bubble formation or limiting their size and quantity, especially in fast tissues.

Ascent speed and DCS

When studying the scallop divers in Maine it is noted that these divers do dives to over 110 ft for as long as they can. They then ride the scallop bucket to the surface (at a rate of around 60 ft/minute) and return for another dive (surface time around five minutes). The divers exceed the US Navy tables by around their second dive, yet complete around 15 to 20 dives in a four hour workday.

Even though DCS is common amongst the divers, there has been no Type II DCS reported and only three spinal DCS cases reported (at the time of the report). The three cases were all due to rapid ascent from depth due to panic or air loss on a single dive. This supports that even with little on-gassing (comparing the single dive to the 15 or 20 dives) incorrect ascent speed can lead to very serious neurological DCS, while slower seems to help protect against CNS DCS.

DAN has data from recreational diver DCS reports that suggest that spinal DCS occurs frequently with fast ascents even when bottom times are only around 20 to 30 minutes at around 60 to 80 ft.

Conclusion

From the above it would seem important to practice gas sharing on occasion to remain in practice (or bailout for CCR divers). It is also important that you constantly monitor your ascent speed and follow your plan correctly. Some divers dive only on computers with no plans, the theory is that the computer calculates decompression in real time. However, it is then very easy to have a too slow ascent speed (most computers warn if you are coming up too fast but none warn for coming up too slowly). This could as noted have the potential of you not having enough gas for decompression or bailout for a CCR diver.

Know where you need to be and at what time and what your expected cylinder gas pressures should be at those times.

Best speed

DAN International with a team of Italian divers did tests to determine the best ascent speed and safety stop time and depth, including deep stop times. Dive depths tested were 25 m (82 ft) for 25 minutes with a total of 181 dives conducted at first and an additional 209 follow up dives conducted to test deep stop time.

From the tests it showed that the best ascent speed was 30 ft/minute, with the best stop depth at ½ the distance for a 2½ minute deep stop and a safety stop at 20 ft for three to five minutes. Ascent rates slower than 20 ft/minute would add significantly to the overall decompression time.

Anton Swanepoel

From the test it was concluded that a one minute stop is not enough time to give the fast tissues time to off-gas enough, and a longer than 2½ minute stop allowed slow tissues to on-gas too much, creating a higher bubble score. It was actually noted that doing a one minute deep stop with a two minute shallow stop was only marginally higher in bubble scores than not making any stops at all.

Since the original suggested ascent rate from the US Navy and UK Navy in 1956 was 60 ft/minute, the recreational community accepted this ascent rate for a long time until it was shown that 30 ft/minute was a more acceptable ascent rate. Before dive computers became standard equipment for most divers, divers were told not to exceed 60 ft/minute or faster than their smallest bubbles, a very exact way of controlling ascent speed, not. ☺

From the DAN tests it showed that slowing down the ascent rate reduced DCS incidence (particularly neurological DCS) and pulmonary barotrauma in recreational divers. It was noted that the shallow stop alone was not as important as the deep stop and the correct ascent rate combined, however it is still advised to do the shallow stop.

It should be noted that the deep stop depth and stop time worked only for this dive set; when the dive is deeper the deep stop in cases produced more bubbles. On shallower dives the deep stop did not seem to make as much of a difference. It would seem then that deep stop depths and times are in some way related to the bottom depth, the time at bottom, the gas breathed and the ascent speed. Now we just need to find the formula. ☺

NAUI has adopted this research and did further study with the help of Dr Bruce Wienke. Thus for NAUI hard tables it is suggested to make a 2½ minute deep stop at half the depth. It is also noted that should a diver do a multilevel dive, then this stop is not needed as this recommendation is only for square profile dives.

Fast ascent rates thus excite fast tissues in possibly forming bubbles, at 30 ft/minute ascent rate the one and possibly two minute half time tissues are not normally at risk, ascents faster than 60 ft/minute would see tissue half times of less than one minute excited, causing short half time tissues such as skin, lung, and brain to be at risk, increasing skin and neurological DCS risk.

Some have the thought that ascent speed should be a % of your depth. This will allow you to have a faster ascent speed from the bottom and gradually slow down as you reach the shallower depths. The theory is that the ascent speed should be linked to tissue loading and pressure difference and not actual depth changes. On the initial ascent the fast tissues control the stops (if any) and as they off-gas quicker and have a higher tolerance for pressure differences, you can make a faster ascent without problems. As slower and slower tissues start to come close to their max pressure difference tolerance you slow the ascent down.

However, here it gets a bit complicated; for the tissue pressure difference is not just related to depth, but also to time spent at depth. Thus it would be difficult to come up with one set of speeds that works for all dives. The problem is also how to judge that you are doing the correct speed. If you select a speed and constantly come up at that speed, it becomes habit and one can reasonably judge (with the help of a dive computer) if you are close to that ascent speed, while constantly changing your ascent speed is operationally difficult.

Swallowing on fast ascent

On a fast ascent, ambient pressure change will be fast, resulting in the gas in the diver's lungs rapidly expanding. Provided the diver exhales at the same rate or faster as the gas expands, the lungs will not be over pressurized. It may be well known that holding your breath can result in lung over expansion injuries, however what will happen if the diver swallows on the way up?

When you swallow your epiglottis closes off and has the same effect as holding your breath. (Try it, swallow, you will feel that you cannot exhale while swallowing). The same happens when you equalize your ears using the Valsalva maneuver. Although most divers know they should not use the method when ascending, divers with ear problems sometimes are so focused on equalizing their ears that they do not realize that they are ascending.

In both cases, if the gas in the lungs expands sufficiently then the lungs can rupture or gas bubbles can be forced into the arterial blood stream, possibly leading to CNS DCS or worse. Although it may not be practical to avoid swallowing, making a slow ascent and watching one's actual depth while equalizing can save you some pain later on.

Note, a person normally swallows automatically every one to five minutes to naturally replace the oxygen that gets absorbed in the inner ears, allowing the ears to equalize. This is a natural response and if not done the pressure will slowly reduce in the inner ears as O2 is absorbed over time. With higher PPO2 breathing the rate of pressure loss may be greater and more frequent swallowing might be needed even with no ambient pressure change.

Descent speed

Note, this section applies to fixed pre-calculated tables or dive plans generated by computer software and written on a slate. A dive computer will adjust decompression and stops in real time.

Many people give lots of attention to ascend speed, yet few give actual attention to descend speed. This may sound unimportant, but let's look at an example and see the results.

If a dive table (fixed or custom cut using software) was created with a descent speed of 50 ft/minute and you descend at 75 ft/minute, then you will reach your bottom depth 50% earlier. If you descend at 100 ft/minute (common on deep drops to save time) you will reach your bottom depth at half the time.

-Descending faster than planned

Taking a dive to 300 ft, at 50 ft/minute one would need six minutes to reach the bottom. If doing a modest OC dive with 20 minutes bottom time, you have only 14 minutes of actual bottom time as six minutes is taken up by the descend. Descending at 100 ft/minute, 300 ft is reached in only three minutes, and if staying till the 20 minute run time, the actual bottom time increases to 17 minutes. This will result in an increase in bottom time of three minutes or 21.4%.

Without knowing it, your custom cut decompression table may now have inadequate decompression time for the dive you did.

A note on descent speed, it was found from tests that the faster the descent speed was (if calculated for in the decompression) the less bubbles were found at decompression. This could be due to nuclei being crushed before inert gas can dissolve into them on the descent (preventing them from being crushed).

Anton Swanepoel

-Descending slower than planned

Some divers use a descent speed of 100 to 200 ft/minute for planning purposes and descend slower than the planned descent rate. When descending slower than the planned descent rate you will have less actual bottom time than calculated by your decompression profile.

Taking the example from before but reversing it, we see that should we plan a dive to 300 ft with a descent rate of 100 ft and an ascent run time of 20 minutes we have an actual bottom time of 17 minutes. If you then descend at only 50 ft/minute the bottom time drops to only 14 minutes. Even though you end the bottom part of the dive at 20 minutes as planned, you are actually ending the dive early.

Descending slower than planned is normally seen as safe as you have on-gassed less than the required decompression is calculated for depending on how far your actual bottom time is out from the calculated bottom time. It is possible that if the bottom time is far enough out, the planned stop depths may be too deep as no compartment would have reached a critical supersaturation at that depth. It may also then happen that the following stops may be incorrect and that you could possibly pass a stop that is now needed but was not calculated for in the original planning, making things worse not safer.

Conclusion

If using tables that are fixed, then find out the descent speed they were calculated for. If using custom cut tables (software such as V-planner), then use the correct or as close as possible actual descent speed that you will drop with. On the dive monitor your progress and increase or decrease your drop rate to match your planned speed. Decompression is not an exact science and not everything is known about it, why introduce another unknown?

How fast can you drop?

Trivia: the Royal Navy did submarine escape tests to see how humans tolerate rapid compression (simulating flooding of a submarine at depth, 20 seconds) followed by rapid decompression to simulate an escape with a buoyancy vest.

In 112 ascents done by 20 men, compression rates of 1476 ft/minute to 150 m (around 500 ft) followed by a decompression rate of 510 ft/minute was tolerated by the men. On deeper tests to 191 m (around 630 ft) with the same speeds, mild itching was reported in a few instances. However, no cases of air embolism or DCS were reported. Five cases of ear squeeze resulting in one case of a perforated tympanic membrane were reported.

BCD type and ascent speed

From studies done on BCD type and configuration, it was noted that the lift of the BCD is not the only factor that affects runaway ascent speeds. It was noted that the location of the bubble (that creates lift) had a marked influence on the ascent rate for a runaway ascent.

BCDs that had the bladder on the back (back mounted) and cause divers to normally be horizontal in the water, were slower due to the diver's position causing drag on ascent. Jacket type BCDs and those that the bladder is over the shoulder cause divers to normally be in a vertical position. These BCDs made a missile out of divers and ascent rates in some exceeded 250 ft/minute.

It was also noted that an ascent had to be arrested at bottom before a runaway occurs, for at a point in the ascent the gas in the BCD will expand faster than the dump valve can allow gas to be vented even if the diver holds the deflate button fully down.

Anton Swanepoel

More gas may be additionally vented if the diver uses multiple dumps at the same time (if incorporated in the BCD) while the diver fully exhales. However, it is doubtful that divers will think about this in a runaway ascent as the diver is normally in a degree of panic.

Chapter 19

Gas content or tissue loading model

This chapter and the following chapter are to serve only as an overview of the two different models used in decompression so as to give the reader a better understanding as to why their decompression stops differ.

The tissue loading model is the earliest model for decompression and has undergone immense testing and changes over the years. These models normally follow a traditional or slightly modified 'Haldanian' approach and the aim is to keep gas supersaturation below a critical value thought to be a trigger point for bubbles to form.

Most of these models assume that gas will stay in a dissolved state all the time so long as the critical supersaturation value is not exceeded. Decompression calculated by these models is near correct as long as most of the tissue gas remains in the dissolved state, however the more gas in free phase in the blood the more the calculated decompression can be incorrect.

Due to these models not being designed with nuclei in mind, they do not tract microbubles or nuclei already formed and thus have conventional decompression stops at a shallower depth than what is now thought to be needed to prevent bubble formation.

One may argue then that these models are a break and mend type of diving where bubbles are allowed to be formed and then later treated at shallower stops. Bubbles in the blood are also thought to be the reason for the need for long decompression stops as they slow down decompression.

Anton Swanepoel

These models normally assume that if bubbles form then the sites for bubble formation are in the tissues or the venous side of the blood. Decompression calculations thus limit the amount of gas dissolved in each theoretical compartment to control a gas phase formation and supersaturation levels to avoid DCS during the ascent.

For these models it does not matter if the model uses one or more tissue compartments and if it is a linear, slab or parallel model, all focus on not exceeding a set supersaturation level. The more tissues tracked in the model however, the more possibilities, yet the basic idea is still the same.

Testing for tissue loading model

Bühlmann did a considerable amount of actual testing to validate the ZH-L16 algorithm, however he used only Nitrogen as an inert gas. Half times for Helium are derived from the Nitrogen values and based on the speculative idea that the relative diffusivity of the gasses is all that matters. The values for Helium are then thus also derived from the Nitrogen half time values and are basically an educated guess.

Bühlmann died before he could test his theories for Helium diffusion rates. The values for Helium appear to be too conservative, and for many years people assumed that decompressions on Helium mixes would be longer than on Nitrogen only mixes. This was due to the results of basing Helium diffusion rates on the formula used for Nitrogen. However it seems that the actual diffusion rate for Helium is much faster than the Bühlmann tables call for. This can in part explain why divers using bubble models can cut 20% or more from the deco of a Bühlmann table and not get decompression sickness. It may not be that the bubble model and deep stops work better, but that the Bühlmann table is too conservative, or both.

The tissue loading model has been shown to be good for a range of diving environments and has adapted to the new concept of stopping deeper. Bühlmann himself added deeper stops by incorporating the two minute compartment. With the add-on of Gradient Factor adjustment the tissue loading model can give close to the same deep stops that bubble models give, however normally with longer shallow deco. This profile is preferred by many tech divers.

Chapter 20

Arterial bubble models

The thought of arterial bubbles is not a new idea, even Haldane thought about it. In his 1908 publication he wrote:

"If small bubbles are carried through the lung capillaries and pass, for instance, to a slowly de-saturating part of the spinal cord, they will there increase in size and may produce serious blockage of the circulation or direct mechanical damage."

From tests done, Hills published his findings in 1971 on arterial bubbles. He was able to show that DCS Type I (limb pain) can be changed to Type II (CNS) by changing from continuous decompression to surface decompression, and was accounted for by arterial bubbles.

Dual phase model

As mentioned, conventional Haldanian models normally assume that there are no bubbles initially and that bubbles only form when a trigger point (pressure difference) was exceeded. With the detection of silent bubbles in divers who did not have DCS, a new way of thinking about bubble formation was needed.

The decompression model now not only had to track dissolved gas, but bubbles already in the system before pressure exposure, thus dual phase models were born.

For dissolved gas, the ambient pressure is reduced as fast as allowed and as much as allowed by the tissues to create the fastest safe off-gassing profile, thus bringing the diver as close to the surface as possible before stopping. For bubble formation, the diver needs to be brought up normally at a slower rate to try and prevent too large a pressure difference between tissue dissolved gas pressure and nuclei or existing bubbles.

By making deeper stops, the nuclei dissolved gas pressure is thought to be reduced faster as the gas inside the nuclei dissolves into surrounding tissue or blood, thus the size of the bubbles is reduced or kept stable, preventing it from enlarging to a size that can cause problems. Models that track both free bubbles and dissolved gas are called bubble models or dual phase.

The arterial bubble models are based on a paper published in 1989 by Hennessy about the physical aspects of the arterial bubbles scenarios and largely focuses on the filtering capacity of the lungs and the fact that bubbles can pass the lungs without being filtered. These bubbles can then later grow on ascent or decompression. Although many models use calculations based on the theory that the threshold size for the bubble to grow is the size of a blood cell and in the range up to 8 μm it should be noted that lung shunts occur where objects up to 100 μm can pass without filtering.

Bubble models have carved a deep niche for themselves in the technical diver community, and algorithms include VPM (varying permeability model) and RGBM (reduced gradient bubble model).

Models calculate for inadequate filtering and start with bubble formation that is thought to be in the vascular bed and later transported by the venous blood to the lungs. Thus since the lungs cannot totally be relied upon to filter out all bubbles, the focus is on preventing bubbles from forming and any existing bubbles from growing, since if bubbles reach a critical size they are either filtered by the lungs or get stuck somewhere in the body.

Testing on bubble models

Although the models are used by many divers, there is little actual testing done on the models, especially using control groups.

It should be noted that there are many ways to decompress, and without actual comparative testing it is impossible to say if one model reduces DCS risk or can actually reduce decompression time without increasing DCS risk.

The notion of feeling fine or better after a dive is subjective - better than what? The dive you did not do on a different decompression schedule, or the dive you did last year where you partied all night before the dive or was up all night getting your gear ready? Alternatively, a host of other factors may cloud your perception of feeling better, including your personal belief that the new dive profile is better. People also have poor memory and may not remember how they felt on the old profile, see the Discovery channel memory test episode for proof, people do not even remember the person that was behind the counter 20 seconds ago (National Geographic, Test your brain, part 1 to 3; Pay attention, Perception and Memory).

In the Discovery show a person would be called from passers by to participate in a test, when the candidate reached the counter the staff behind the counter informed them they just needed to get a pen and ducked down behind the counter.

A different staff member then appeared a few seconds later serving the candidate. Very few people actually noticed the change. When the original staff member was later brought to the candidate, many denied ever seeing the staff member, until they were shown a recording of the events.

-What works works

What works works may work, but is it the best or better than the rest? This is not to discredit the dives or models, just a note that it should be seen as a step towards better decompression models as we learn more. Yes it is costly, but more tests are needed before any claims can be made.

What works may also not actually work. It was noted from reports that large differences in reported DCS cases were seen in tunnel workers using the same tables on different sites, from 0.54 to 6.4% DCS reported on the same tables. It was found that improper use of the tables (possibly to increase productivity or misunderstanding of the use of the tables) led to the large DCS reported differences.

The opposite is often the case with non commercial technical divers. Divers often pad final decompression stops for increased safety in addition to breathing the highest deco mix on the surface before exiting the water. To say the algorithm is correct on the basis that the diver did not get DCS may be incorrect as the additional padding and deco breathing on the surface could have fixed a failure in the calculations.

An additional note, it is known that to reduce the risk of DCS, a large increase in decompression is needed to reduce the risk a very small percentage. On the flip side, a large amount of decompression can sometimes be dropped while only increasing the risk marginally compared to the amount of decompression omitted.

From tests done by the US Navy on divers to 170 ft for 30 minutes, it was calculated that a 174 minute decompression time would yield a 6% DCS risk, while reducing the decompression to 48 minutes would only increase the risk to around 8 or 9%.

Anton Swanepoel

It should also be noted that in bubble detection, bubbles can only be detected by Doppler if they are moving, stationary bubbles do not show. Bubbles that are too small for the device to detect may also exist.

Those that believe that all is ok as they feel ok or "better" after a dive with some adjusted profile should take a note on studies on tunnel workers and long-term damage. In one such study in 1965 Rozsahgyi reported that 42% of Hungarian tunnel workers that never had CNS DCS had abnormal electroencephalograms (brain activity). Bone necrosis is also reported to be common in tunnel workers (less now due to better decompression tables). Bone necrosis may result from only one inadequate decompression even if no DCS symptoms occurred.

Symptoms such as headache and fatigue in the immediate post dive are also probably symptoms of subclinical DCI and some might think that because they are not associated with overt symptoms of DCI, they are not causing any damage thus no need to worry. Ever seen an iceberg? Nine tenths of the damage may be invisible and cumulative.

Chapter 21

M-values

M-values (Maximum values) like Gradient Factors (explained in following chapters) are some of the most widely used terms in decompression. However, most divers do not even have a high level understanding of what either is.

Following is an overlook at what M-values are to prepare the reader for the calculation on Deep Stops and Gradient Factors in the following chapters. Note for readers who have bought my book 'Dive Computers', some of the information is a repeat, however this chapter is more an overview of M-values in preparation for the calculations in the Gradient Factor chapter, where the computer book has more examples in for an explanation of how M-values work and how decompression is calculated.
www.antonswanepoelbooks.com/dive_computers.php

The term "M-value" was coined by US Navy Captain (NEDU) Robert D Workman (mid 1960s) while doing research on decompression for the US Navy Experimental Diving Unit.

Different body tissues are assigned a diffusion value or half time (M-value). This value, expressed in minutes, is the amount of time that a compartment takes to on- or off-gas half the difference in pressure between the gasses dissolved inside the compartment and those outside. Fast compartments include the brain and spinal column; medium compartments include muscle tissue; and slower compartments include fat and bone.

It takes about six half times for a compartment to fill to a level that is assumed to be in equilibrium with the surrounding pressure, although the pressure is actually slightly less.

Anton Swanepoel

Most dive models will have an amount of gas compartments that it uses in its calculations. The number of compartments and their half life values affect the dive time and decompression they will predict.

At sea level, the tissues are saturated with a total pressure of around 1 atm (around 0.21 ata O2 and 0.745 ata N2, excluding trace gasses), note water vapor was deducted from the N2 pressure. As you descend the ambient pressure increases and so too inspired gas pressure. Around every 33 fsw (10 msw) the ambient pressure increases another 1 atm. Thus at 33 fsw the inspired pressure for air would be around 0.42 ata O2 and 1.58 ata N2 (N2 pressure increases as tank air has water vapor removed).

Each tissue will take on gas at its own rate depending on the tissue type and the blood flow to it until it is in equilibrium with the pressure of the inert gas in the blood surrounding it, called saturation. When you ascend the ambient pressure will be reduced and so too the inspired gas pressure. Depending on the half-life of the tissue, different tissues (faster ones first) will start to have a higher pressure in the tissue than the surrounding blood, called supersaturation. The difference in pressure between the inert gas in a tissue and that of the inspired gas is the pressure ratio, gradient or M-value.

It was found that different tissue half lifes could handle a different pressure ratio, including that this ratio differed depending on the current depth. Thus, for a given tissue and ambient pressure, the M-value is the maximum difference in inert gas pressure that a hypothetical tissue is thought to be able to tolerate without overt symptoms of DCS.

Both Bühlmann and Workman came up with formulas to work this out. Bühlmann's M-values are some of the most widely used, in part due to a number of books he published on the subject of decompression.

Since the maximum pressure ratio that a compartment could tolerate without bubble formation is linked to its half-time and current depth, a closely linear line can be drawn from the bottom to the surface as a safe ceiling for decompression. As long as the inert gas pressure in each tissue for each half life is below this line all should be fine. Bühlmann derived two factors, calling them 'a' and 'b', the 'a' value can be seen as the lower anchor point at the start of the ascent for the linear line, and the 'b' value can be seen as the anchor point for the endpoint (surface) for the linear line.

Note that each compartment has its own pair of 'a' and 'b' values. The 'a' and 'b' modifiers are obtained from the following formula:

$$a = 2 \times tht^{-1/3}$$
$$b = 1.005 - tht^{-1/2}$$

Where:
tht = the half-time (M-value) for the compartment.

For example, the values for the 12.5 minute compartment are:
a = 2 x 12.5$^{-1/3}$ = 0.8618 and b = 1.005 – 12.5$^{-1/2}$ = 0.7222

Once the 'a' and 'b' value for each M-value is found it can be used to calculate the maximum pressure difference that a tissue can tolerate, and thus the minimum depth the diver can ascend to, this will be covered in the next chapter called 'Deep Stops'.

Anton Swanepoel

For each tissue half life, the amount of inert gas on- and off-gassed in a given period of time is done using the following formula:

Bühlmann diffusion formula

$$P_{comp} = P_{begin} + [\ P_{gas} - P_{begin}\ ] \times [\ 1 - 2^{\ -t_e/t_{ht}}\ ]$$

Where:

P_{begin} = Inert gas pressure in the compartment before the exposure time in bar.

P_{comp} = Inert gas pressure in the compartment after the exposure time in bar.

P_{gas} = Inert gas pressure in the mixture being breathed in bar.

t_e = Length of the exposure time in minutes.

t_{ht} = Half time of the compartment.

The calculations need to be done for every compartment that the model uses.

For example a dive to 140 ft for 25 minutes on air using a 4 and 12.5 minute half life compartment:

The Nitrogen pressure is $((140 / 33) + 1) * 0.79 = 4.1415$ atm, staring pressure is 0.745 ata as water vapor is deducted, see 'Dive Computers' book for more detail and calculations.

4 minute compartment:
$P_{comp} = 0.745 + [4.1415 - 0.745] \times [1 - 2^{\ -25/4}]$
$P_{comp} = 0.745 + [3.3965] \times [0.9868609935]$
$= 4.09688$ atm ending N2 pressure.

12.5 minute compartment:
$P_{comp} = 0.745 + [4.1415 - 0.745] \times [1 - 2^{\ -25/12.5}]$
$P_{comp} = 0.745 + [3.3965] \times [0.75]$
$= 3.292375$ atm ending N2 pressure.

These values will be used to calculate the first stop if needed on ascent. Although only two compartments are used in the example many algorithms use 8 to 16 or more compartments and the calculations need to be done for each compartment on its own.

To work out the maximum pressure difference a compartment can handle and find the minimum depth we can ascend to before we need to make a decompression stop the following formula from Bühlmann is used:

$$P_{amb.tol} = (P_{comp} - a) \times b$$

Where:

P_{comp} = the inert gas pressure in the compartment.

$P_{amb.tol}$ = the pressure you could drop to, given as absolute pressure. Thus 3 bar = 20 m or 66 ft.

a and b = the 'a' and 'b' values for that compartment and the gas in question.

Note values are from the 140 ft dive already calculated before.
4 minute compartment:
$P_{amb.tol}$ = (4.09688 – 1.2599) x 0.5050 = 1.4326345 atm
1.4326345 – 1 = 0.4326345 * 33 = 14.3 ft

12.5 minute compartment:
$P_{amb.tol}$ = (3.292375 - 0.8618) x 0.7222 = 1.755361265 atm
1.755361265 – 1 = 0.755361265 * 33 = 24.93 ft

As can be seen, according to the Bühlmann calculations we need our first stop at 25 ft. This compartment controls the dive on this example. Note this is only true if using only these two compartments as will be seen in the next chapter 'Deep Stops'.

Chapter 22

Deep Stop calculations

After all the talk of deep stops, one may wonder how to calculate deep stops. That is part of the problem about deep stops, for there are a number of ways to do it. If you are using a computer, tables or computer software that incorporates deep stops into the algorithm then deep stops will be calculated for you. If you are not using any of these, or want to add additional deep stops, here are a few ways it can be done.

If dive tables or computers were to only use one fixed ratio, then there would only be one compartment controlling the dive depending on the depth. However, if the model uses different ratios for different compartments, multiple compartments will control the dive at different depths.

From the previous chapter we noted that when using a 4 and 12.5 minute compartment we needed to make the first stop at 25 ft. Bühlmann did introduce the two minute compartment with its own 'a' and 'b' modifiers to alter the profile so that deeper stops are made.

Example

We will use the dive to 140 ft for 25 minutes on air from the previous chapter but with the two minute compartment for deep stop calculation. The same calculations still need to be done for all other compartments. 140 ft the Nitrogen pressure is 4.1415 atm Nitrogen.

Pressure ratio deep stop calculation:

If we do not want to exceed a pre calculated pressure to prevent bubbles from forming, at what depth would the two minute compartment reach this ratio? Discount off-gassing on ascent and using 1.58:1 ratio, we have 4.1415 / 1.58 = 2.6212 atm

Since this 2.6212 atm is Nitrogen pressure only, the depth pressure is 2.6212 / 0.79 = 3.318. This is equal to (3.318 -1) * 33 = 77 ft. Note that some models use a lower ratio than 1.58:1 for micro bubble stops and will cause the first stop to be deeper.

Richard Pyle deep stop calculation:
((Max depth – first deco stop) / 2) + first deco stop
((200 – 25) /2) + 25 = 113 ft (first deco stop already calculated)

Bühlmann ZH-L17B tissue compartment 0 with 2 min half life for deep stop calculations and 'a' and 'b' values = '0.3', '0.83'
$P_{amb.tol}$ = (4.1415 - 0.3) x 0.83 = 3.19 atm
= 3.19 – 1 = 2.19 * 33 = 73 ft (rounded)

As we can see, the two minute compartment created a deeper stop than either the 4 or 12.5 minute compartments due to its 'a' and 'b' modifiers.

For the next stop we will use the middle value of 77 ft.

The distance from 140 to 77 ft is 63 ft. Thus it will take the diver around two minutes to reach 77 ft. The pressure difference is 4.1415 – 2.63 = 1.515. However, since the diver takes two minutes to reach 77 ft, he/she does not have that difference for the entire two minutes. We can say that he/she has half the difference as an average for the two minutes. Thus the diver off-gasses:

P_{comp} = 4.1415 - [1.515 / 2] x [1 – 2$^{-2/2}$]
P_{comp} = 4.1415 - [0.7575] x [0.5]
= 3.76275 atm Nitrogen still left in the two minute compartment.

After two minutes deep stop:
P_{comp} = 3.76275 - [3.76275 - 2.63333] x [1 – 2$^{-2/2}$]
P_{comp} = 3.76275 - [1.12942] x [0.5]
= 3.19804 atm Nitrogen still left in the two minute compartment.

Anton Swanepoel

We can now ascend to a shallower depth.

Ratio deep stop:
Using a rough calculation again and disregarding the loss of pressure on ascent, we see that the next stop for this compartment is 3.19804 / 1.58 = 2.02408 atm / 0.79 atm.
(2.5622 – 1) * 33 = 52 ft

Richard Pyle deep stop calculation:
(Stop depth – first deco stop) / 2
((77 – 25) /2) + 25 = 51 ft (almost the same as ratio stops)

Bühlmann calculations:
$P_{amb.tol}$ = (3.19804 - 0.3) x 0.83 = 2.4054 atm
= 2.4054 – 1 = 1.4054 * 33 = 47 ft

You would continue adding the stops until you are within 33 ft (10 m) from your first original decompression stop.

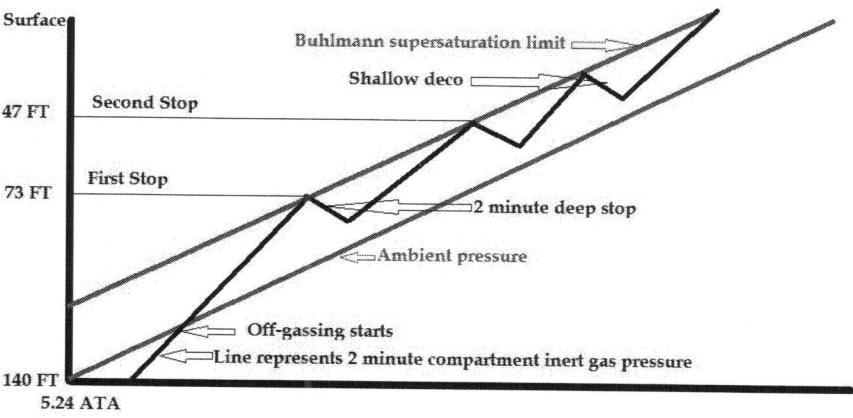

Risk of adding stops too deep

As can be seen from the example, the deco stops are calculated using the inert gas pressure in the tissues for each M-value. Each tissue will have an inert gas loading, this pressure will be equal to a depth value. Thus any tissue that has not saturated at depth before the ascent will have an inert gas pressure that is equal to a shallower depth.

Example:
If we still use the two minute compartment but only stay six minutes, the compartment will not be saturated.
P_{comp} = 0.745 + [4.1415 – 0.745] x [1 – 2 $^{-6/2}$]
P_{comp} = 0.745 + [3.3965] x [0.875]
= 3.71523925 atm will be the pressure. This is equal to:
3.71523925 – 1 = 2.71523925 * 33 = 89.6 ft

If you add a deep stop deeper than 90 ft the compartment and any slower compartments will on-gas more inert gas instead of off-gassing.

When using a computer the computer will keep on calculating as you dive, thus if adding a stop as mentioned above, the computer will calculate the additional inert gas uptake and recompute any stops needed. However, if you use tables then the added inert gas may require a deeper stop than your table gives as it was not designed with the stops you added. Doing this may invalidate your decompression and add to DCS risk.

Many dive computers use the Bühlmann formula to calculate stops but just modify the 'a' and 'b' modifiers to create deeper stops and longer decompression for safety, called Gradient Factors.

Anton Swanepoel

Chapter 23

Gradient Factors

Computers allowing you to change the M (maximum) values or Gradient Factors for the compartments normally express them as GF low and GF high, although a new algorithm has recently been released allowing you to change the mid factors or mid level stops. The Bühlmann ascent line is a supersaturation gradient line that is calculated at the maximum supersaturation any tissue can handle before bubbles are thought to form. The GF line is a line that either follows the Bühlmann ascent line or is below it depending on the settings used.

Changing the GF low will influence the first decompression stops, and changing the GF high will influence the surface value and as such the last decompression stops and times.

A Gradient Factor of 1 is the same as a Bühlmann M-value, and a Gradient Factor of 0 is when your compartment reaches ambient pressure. Thus setting a Gradient Factor of 0.8 is 80% of Bühlmann's values and gives you a 20% safety over his values.

If you set your GF low to let's say 0.2, your computer will let you ascend not allowing your compartments to exceed 20% of the distance between ambient pressure and Bühlmann's M-value (calculated for each tissue compartment used separately).

The GF high is the maximum distance between ambient pressure and Bühlmann's M-value that you can surface with. Setting the value to 0.8 your computer will create stops and not allow you to surface with a pressure ratio exceeding 80% than what the standard Bühlmann table would have allowed you to surface with.

Note that when using Helium in the gas mixture, you need to use a computer that can calculate the off-gassing rate of Helium, as it differs from Nitrogen (although many believe you can dive with up to 15% Helium and use standard air tables, as the Helium off-gasses faster and the table will give more deco than is needed).

The idea with Gradient Factors is to first ascend with a lower Gradient Factor then slowly get closer to the Bühlmann values as you near the surface. The GF low would then be the value you start with and the GF high would be your ending value against Bühlmann's value. The sliding value that constantly increases is called the GF max. This value starts off the same as the GF low and ends the same value as the GF high. It should be noted that an anchor point is needed to anchor the GF line.

The anchor point is the point where the GF max is the same as the GF high. This point is normally set at the surface, thus you would surface with a pressure difference not exceeding your GF high point against Bühlmann values. If the anchor point is set at 15 ft, then you will reach 15 ft with a pressure difference not exceeding your GF high point against Bühlmann values but would surface with Bühlmann values.

Since the GF low is the first stop depth and the GF high is the anchor point, you can draw a line from the first stop to the anchor point. So long as you stay below or on that line you are ok according to the algorithm used.

Since the gradient changes as you ascend from your low setting to your high setting, we need to calculate what the new factor would be for each subsequent stop depth we want to go to.

Anton Swanepoel

The following calculations are not 100% correct as off-gassing on ascent and other variables are not incorporated in order to make the calculations easier to understand, and serve only for academic purpose to help the reader understand Gradient Factors.

From the previous chapter we saw that on the two minute compartment the first stop was 73 ft.

GF deep
To calculate the GF deep stop we use the following modified Bühlmann formula with an initial GF of 0.2 (GF set to 20/80).
$P_{amb.tol}$ = (P i.g. - GF * a) / (GF/b - GF + 1)
(4.1415 – 0.2 * 0.3) / (0.2 / 0.83 – 0.2 +1)
= 3.921 (rounded) – 1 = 2.921 * 33 = 97 ft (rounded up)

Note:
For those that wonder what the formula does, there is another way of explaining it, although the results and calculations are slightly different and not totally correct, shown here just for academic purpose only.

The supersaturation allowed was 4.1415 - 3.19 = 0.9515 atm. Note, the 4.1415 is Nitrogen only pressure while the 3.19 is absolute ambient pressure as the formula calculates the amount of supersaturation for an inert gas against ambient pressure. Since we are only allowed an initial 20% of that pressure difference we can only ascend until the tissues are supersaturated with 20% of that pressure difference.
0.9515 atm * 20% = 0.1903. Thus our first stop will be 4.1415 - 0.1903 = 3.9512 atm – 1 = 2.9512 * 33 = 97 ft (rounded)

If we do a two minute stop and disregard off-gassing on the ascent we will lose:

After two minutes deep stop:
P_{comp} = 4.1415 - [4.1415 – 3.1121] x [1 – 2 $^{-2/2}$]
P_{comp} = 4.1415 - [1.0294] x [0.5]
= 3.6268 atm N2 pressure in compartment

Using Bühlmann calculation again:
$P_{amb.tol}$ = (3.6268 - 0.3) x 0.83 = 2.761244 atm
= 2.761244 – 1 = 1.761244 * 33 = 58 ft (rounded), this would have been our next stop without GF.

GF max
Now we have to work out what the GF max would be for this depth (this is the sliding GF value).

GF max = GF High – (((GF High – GF low) / last stop) * new stop)
GF max = 0.80 – (((0.80 – 0.2) / 97) * 58)
GF max = 0.8 – 0.3588
GF max = 0.4412 or 44.12%
Using this new value we alter our deep stop.

(3.6268 – 0.4412 * 0.3) / (0.4412/ 0.83 – 0.4412 +1)
= 3.205 (rounded) – 1 = 2.205 * 33 = 73 ft (rounded up)

Let's see how far our second calculation differs from the formula:
We had a pressure difference of 3.6268 - 2.761244 = 0.86556 atm
0.86556 atm * 44.12% = 0.38188 atm
3.6268 - 0.38188 atm = 3.24492 atm
3.24492 atm – 1 = 2.24492 * 33 = 74 ft (rounded), 1 ft difference

Note, the two minute compartment with two minute stops allowed us a 24 ft step up. The shorter the stop time per deep stop is the closer the next depth will be as you will not have off-gassed that much and is the reason why the stops get longer and longer the shallower you get due to slower and slower tissues starting to control the stops.

Anton Swanepoel

We also note the effect of making the conservatism too high. The stops are deep and close together, causing the diver to spend more time deep. This time deep could allow other tissues to on-gas more inert gas that has a penalty on decompression later, causing longer stops.

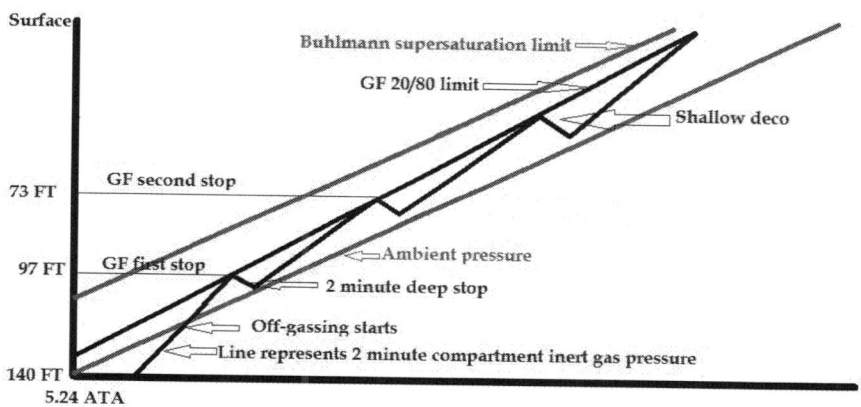

Note that only one tissue was used in the example, the two minute tissue. These calculations need to be done for all the tissues in the algorithm as another tissue will have a deeper stop depth as you go shallower.

An additional note on inert gas fraction changes, when you change to a different mix, the off-gassing may increase and allow you to ascend to a shallower stop faster.

From the calculations it would be obvious how hard it is to calculate Gradient Factors for rebreathers as the PPO2 constantly changes. And where do you anchor the last stop? Normally it is anchored at the surface, but do you anchor it at 15 ft or do you anchor it at the surface? There is also a problem with CCR divers flushing their units on shallower stops, sending the PPO2 all over the place, as a dive computer or table manufacturer how do you deal with that?

In the picture on page 163 the anchor point is the surface, thus the line will end with 80% of the pressure difference given by the Bühlmann calculations. The lower the GF low is the deeper the stop and the more the ascent is slowed down.

Chapter 24

Yo yo dives

Yo yo diving is the name given to a pattern of diving where divers make repeated dives to depth with very short surface intervals. Dives are normally inside no decompression times and can include a safety stop or not. These dive profiles are normally made by fish farming (removing dead fish), dive instructors (teaching new divers and making multiple ascents), film crew, and sometimes beginner divers.

Divers may quickly pop to the surface to grab additional tools when working underwater, give instructions to new divers or do emergency ascent tests, make an accidental surface (possibly new diver or rusty diver who had not dived in a while), and lost divers who pop to the surface to get their bearings to the boat or shore.

The thought is that so long as the total bottom time fits inside a single dive's bottom time for no decompression limits then going to the surface repeatedly is ok, however this theory does not account for any bubble formation. It should be noted that many no decompression limits do not protect the brain and is the reason for a safety stop. The ascents on most tables are too fast to protect the brain and if a safety stop is omitted there is added risk for brain bubbles.

Most repetitive tables also do not account for the possibility of bubbles and how that might affect off-gassing.

Computers and yo yo diving

It was shown in reports from Shield and reports by Unimed Scientific Ltd for the Health and Safety Executive (2004) that yo yo diving if done correctly (with safety stops) and in shallower waters on tables can be safer than a single dive with the same bottom time.

More cases have been found of DCS in yo yo diving where the diver used a dive computer than tables. This may be due to the added dive time a dive computer gives compared to tables for multilevel dives. A study into fish farming dive profiles revealed that the practices performed there were quite safe even though many dives were reverse profile (shallow dive followed by deeper dive) and yo yo bounce dives. However, it should be noted that the dives were to shallow depths with slow ascent rates and most used safety stops.

Staying with slow ascent rates and making a safety stop is seen to be extremely important for yo yo diving. As the brain is seen to be at the greatest risk due to the fast tissues, any bubbles that do form will be compressed on subsequent dives and can cause problems, however any bubbles that do form may grow on surface intervals and the longer a surface interval is the larger a bubble may grow. It was found that for many dives, the relation of bottom time to surface interval is around 1:10. Thus for every minute of bottom time, the diver needs around 10 minutes of surface time to clear the gas that was taken up.

Thus on repetitive dives the slower tissues may accumulate more gas than a computer algorithm calculates and the safe bottom times indicated by the computer may not be correct as computers are not normally designed for yo yo diving, however the tissue half time used for repetitive diving even in tables is a major factor.

Anton Swanepoel

When PADI created the new recreational dive planner, they decided to drop the use of the 120 minute tissue compartment that the US Navy tables used and use the 60 minute tissue compartment instead for a limiting compartment on repetitive dives as recreational divers do shorter but more dives than the Navy divers (initially the 40 minute compartment was used as a limiting compartment on repetitive dives but proved too short for long shallow dives).

In the test phase two program, doing six dives a day and staying in the table limits, a DCS incident on day two caused that regime to be abandoned and the conclusion made that six dives a day is too much. Therefore, it is suggested that only three to four dives be made on the PADI tables per day with a rest day (reduced diving or none) every two to three days.

Note, although the tables use 14 compartments, from 5 minutes to 480 minutes, it is the 60 minute compartment used as a limiting compartment in repetitive dives that proved too short when doing four or more dives a day for multi day diving.

Conclusion for yo yo diving

Our understanding of the risks of yo yo diving is then not totally correct. If done correctly with slow ascents and safety stops it can be safer than one dive with the same bottom time as the multiple dives and surface time combined. For example, one dive to 60 ft for 55 minutes compared to two dives of 25 minutes each and a 5 minute surface interval.

Diving deeper on the second dive itself is not the problem, but the speed of ascent and the duration of the bottom time. Remember any part of the second dive below the surface is actually deeper than some part of the first dive and if a short bounce dive with rapid ascent is done even if to a shallow depth bubbles may form.

Chapter 25

Conclusion

So where does all of this talk leave us?

We noted that decompression is a very complex subject that is not fully understood and currently handled by many theories, some tested some not.

We noted that many factors can influence the outcome of the same dive profile (depth and time), thermal changes in water, ascent speed, first stop depth, individual susceptibility, gasses breathed, and many more.

It was also noted that slowing the ascent and stopping deeper (20 ft against 15 ft) seemed to reduce bubbles for recreational divers.

For technical decompression (non saturation) dives (especially tri-mix) dives there seems to be convincing evidence that a slower ascent (30 ft against 60 ft) and making deeper first stops (compared to straight Bühlmann calculations) may reduce bubble formation in certain dives. However, inserting deeper stops can come at a penalty with additional decompression time. In addition, inserting stops too deep and too many stops may cause very long shallow decompression. If not calculating for the added decompression (not assuming a bubble model that may give credit for deeper stops) then there could be added DCS risk.

The reader is thus urged to make a careful decision when deciding to follow any algorithm and to know the shortcomings of the chosen algorithm including the possible effects of altering an algorithm.

Anton Swanepoel

Food for thought, in June 2008 the Undersea Hyperbaric Medical Society (UHMS) organized a workshop in America where some of the top people in decompression research came together to discuss deep stops. The result of the workshop (two days) was the conclusion that currently we really do not know and more research is needed. In the workshop book from the proceedings ("Decompression and the Deep Stop Workshop Proceedings" ISBN 0-930406-24-9) the following statement was made:

"In respect of decompression diving there is conflicting evidence regarding the relative efficacy of decompression regimens that include empirical or model-derived deep stops (as defined) and decompression regimes prescribed by gas content models."

If the top people in the diving decompression world do not know, are you sure you know what you know is correct?

Many algorithms are guesses following theories of on- and off-gassing, changing that willy nilly is silly. ☺

End note

Thank you for the purchase of this book. May it help you to find relieve from ear pain and some restful sleep in addition to keeping you ears pain free on your journey through life.

For comments please e-mail me at antonswanepoel@yahoo.com For bulk purchases and discount for resellers, please e-mail info@antonswanepoelbooks.com

Anton Swanepoel

For More information and free sample downloads of other books by me, including news on books currently in progress visit www.antonswanepoelbooks.com

Be sure to check out the free stuff page that is loaded with free books from writing tips, weight loss, health tips and more.

Resources

Webpages
http://www.cavediver.net
http://www.thefullwiki.org
http://www.southpacificdivers.com
http://technical-sidemount.com
http://www.scubamonster.com
http://plongee-tech.pagesperso-orange.fr
http://retis.sssup.it
http://ajwatts.co.uk
http://www.direxplorers.com
http://www.pure-tech-agency.net
http://www.cognitas.org.uk
http://rubicon-foundation.org
http://jap.physiology.org
http://pages.uoregon.edu/lovering/lab/index.html
http://www.jmvh.org

Workshops
The Physiological Basis of Decompression (Undersea Hyperbaric Medical Society) Proceeding 38
Biomechanics of Safe Ascents (American Academy of Underwater Science, 1989)

People
Charlie Christiansen

Spelling and grammar
Toni McNally
Ginger It! Spelling and grammar Software
WhiteSomke 2012 plus, spelling and grammar software

Other Books by this Author

For a complete list of books by the author and more details on each book see
www.antonswanepoelbooks.com/books.php

The Art of Gas Blending
www.antonswanepoelbooks.com/the_art_of_gas_blending.php

This is an excellent must have book for any gas blender, Technical diver or person interested in technical diving, whether you intend to blend gas or not.

Taking on the Road, Two Wheels at a Time
www.antonswanepoelbooks.com/taking_on_the_road.php

Traveling by motorcycle is far different than any other means of transport. In a car, you are always a passenger, seeing a movie of the road going by. On a bike you become one with it, the road and your surrounding is no longer a movie, it's a part of you. For you feel every corner, every bump and your body flexes in harmony with the bike's suspension. You smell the flowers, earth and rain, feel the wind and hear birds as you go, *you are alive.*

This book aims to help you prepare for your next adventure or your first, from down to the pub races, breakfast runs, multiple weeklong rallies, or yearlong multi country travel. From gear selection, packing right, understanding your bike and setting the suspension right to maintenance on the road.

The Art of Travel
www.antonswanepoelbooks.com/the_art_of_travel.php

Travelling is more than just reaching your destination; it's the journey in its totality. Travel is about growing as a person.

Pre-planning, gear selection, backpacks, tents, sleeping bags, boots, clothing, flashlights, GPS devices, pickpocketing, robbery, abduction, date rape drugs, protecting your food in the wild, keeping the crawlers out of your sleeping bag at night, and tips to help you with sticky situations along the way, are all covered in depth.

New adventures and friends are out there, what are you waiting for?

Gas Blender Program

www.antonswanepoelbooks.com/gas_blender_program.php

A step by step guide to creating your own gas blender program in Excel.

This book will show you how to write a blender program in Excel step by step with the values needed for every cell and function. No need to be a programmer, just type in the values from each step.

The program will run on most devices that support spreadsheets, from computers, laptops, smart phones, palms, and iPhones.
Calculations for Nitrox, Tri-Mix, Helair, Heliox, EAD and END are covered, in addition to calculations for actual rebreather loop at depth and END included.

Dive Computers

www.antonswanepoelbooks.com/dive_computers.php

The purpose and aim of this book is to help you in understanding how dive computers work, including calculations on decompression stops, deep stops, ascend ceilings, on- and off gassing, RGBM, VPM and gradient factors.

Sea and Motion Sickness

http://www.antonswanepoelbooks.com/motion_sickness.php

In this book, we will look at what motion sickness is, space sickness, virtual environment sickness, and sea sickness, their causes and triggers, with advice for preventing and treating them. Included in the book is ginger, antihistamine medication, wrist bands, natural herbs, behavior adaption and a lot more, all helping you travel without motion sickness.

Ear Pain

http://www.antonswanepoelbooks.com/ear_pain.php

There are a few different causes of ear pain, and the treatment for each may differ. Understanding why your ears hurt is the first step in finding the off switch to the pain and preventing it from coming on again. Some of the topics covered are: ear pain due to barotrauma, swimmer's ear, surfer's ear, jogging and waterskiing, cold in the ear, airplane ear, ear infection, Tinnitus and referred pain from a tooth abscess. From causes, prevention, to treatment in detail. Additional included is over 10 ways to equalize your ears.

Writing and Publishing Your Own Book

http://www.antonswanepoelbooks.com/writing_and_publishing.php

Change your words from 'I am going', to 'I have written a book'
You can be a writer, for it's a skill learnable by most people. Being a writer is not only a dream for the select few, it's within most people's ability.
In this book I will show you the steps to start and finish writing your book, including publishing and selling it. If you already have books written, you can use the tips to enhance old books and improve future books.

See www.antonswanepoelbooks.com for more details.

2785983R00091

Printed in Great Britain
by Amazon.co.uk, Ltd.,
Marston Gate.